STORAGE

DO NOT REMOVE
CARDS FROM POCKET

ARCO'S
Career
Guidance
Series

Your Career In
PUBLIC RELATIONS

Bob Weinstein

ARCO PUBLISHING, INC.
NEW YORK

For Bonnie

Published by Arco Publishing, Inc.
215 Park Avenue South, New York, N.Y. 10003

Library of Congress Cataloging in Publication Data

Weinstein, Bob, 1941–
    Your career in public relations.

    (Arco's career guidance series)
    Includes index.
    1. Public relations—Vocational guidance—United
States. I. Title. II. Series.
HM263.W436 1982   659.2'023'73   82-3891
ISBN 0-668-05555-3 (Reference Text)
ISBN 0-668-05562-6 (Paper Edition)

Printed in the United States of America

Contents

Acknowledgments

Special thanks to George Nobbe, executive editor of *Real World*, and Lynne Peel, for providing valuable information and assistance in preparing the manuscript; Jenny Weinstein, for transcribing miles of tape; and Josh Weinstein, for constructing graphs and statistical workups.

Introduction

Some careers can be described neatly, with a few crisp well-formed sentences. Not public relations, however. Not that the work is so difficult to define. The problem is it has so many applications.

The best way to get a feeling for what this exciting field is all about is to back into it. That way, you'll have a clear idea of how PR workers get their messages across to the public.

Let's start with an imaginary company we'll call the International Widget Company. At this very moment the company's employees are in a frenzy. In two weeks International Widget is planning to introduce a new brand of widget, which promises to be big news for widget users worldwide. The company has poured over five million dollars into researching and developing a super widget, a new streamlined, disposable widget which, it is hoped, will turn the widget market upside down.

As you might expect, the company's top brass is tense, excited and apprehensive over the upcoming event. Everything is riding on the new product. The tension at corporate headquarters is so thick you can cut it with a knife. The president of the company is riding herd on everyone. Corporate memorandums concerning the new widget are raining down from the executive suite like randomly fired machine gun bullets.

But the burden of breaking the news to the public and media falls on International Widget's public relations staff. In preparation for the big event, public relations workers have been putting in long hours.

1

Why all the excitement and why is the company's top brass stalking the halls as if the world were coming to an end? For good reasons.

Producing the new widget is only the first step. The big problem is telling the world about it and convincing consumers that the new widget is *the* best on the market, rendering all prior models obsolete.

That explains why the company's chief executive can't sit still. Developing the product took time and cost the company a great deal of money. For the past five years International Widget has been growing impressively. The stock has been edging up at a respectable clip and the company's corps of investors is happy with the progress the company has made. But in spite of the company's steady growth, International Widget could just as easily slip into an earnings decline if the new widget doesn't sell well. Not only would the company lose an enormous amount of money, but it might lose credibility as well.

If you think the company's president is nervous, you should see the public relations staff. The company's small, eight-person department has the challenging job of telling the world about the new widget. How they accomplish that could mean either initial acceptance or rejection of the product.

As the senior PR writer in a large cosmetics company put it: "A public relations executive's goal is to capture the public and hold its attention long enough to get across an important message, whatever that may be. It doesn't matter how it's accomplished, as long as it's done effectively, professionally and with lasting impact."

What exactly do *effectively* and *lasting impact* mean? Simply, just telling people about a product is not enough. It could go in one ear and out the other. The challenge for a public relations worker is arousing the public's curiosity and getting its attention so it's motivated to go out and actually try the product. If that can be accomplished, they've managed to hit a well-placed ball into center field, conquering first and second base in the process.

International Widget's public relations staff has developed a couple of overlapping strategies to introduce the product. Seven days before the announcement of the super widget, news releases will be sent to the media telling them about the product and inviting them to a press conference on the scheduled release day. That's not all. On the release date, the public relations staff, working closely with the company's advertising agency, plans to debut television and radio ads on the new widget, spaced at strategic intervals throughout the day and evening. The PR director is leaving nothing to chance. By skillfully promoting the product he hopes it will gain acceptance. He knows all too well that a poorly planned public relations campaign could spell disaster. Disaster means a monumental financial setback for the company. And on a personal level, our PR director could lose his job if the planned campaign fails dismally.

Now you can see how important public relations work is and why we chose this example, rather than struggling to come up with a concise definition.

1

What Is Public Relations?

Most medium-to-large-sized companies maintain public relations staffs. Even small companies are hiring one- and two-person public relations staffs. When a tiny company can't afford a full-time public relations worker, it's not uncommon for the owner or one of the executives to operate in a dual role and perform public relations tasks along with other responsibilities. If that's not possible, the company might retain the services of a freelance public relations person to coordinate PR programs when needed.

It's only in the past 40 years that companies (large and small) have incorporated public relations concepts into their promotional strategies. Of the 300 top companies in the mid-1930's, for example, approximately 1 out of 50 had public relations departments. And now well over 5,000 companies either have public relations departments of their own or retain the services of a PR agency.

Getting People's Attention

One of the most important functions of a public relations worker is getting people's attention. This sounds easy, but in a world where satellites can bring about instantaneous communication to all parts of the world and radio and television are a fact of life, the com-

4

munication process has become easier and more complicated all at the same time. Since so many different forms of communication are vying for our attention, getting someone's attention can be a real challenge.

In the early 1900's, for example, the communication process was a lot simpler. Cities were just beginning to grow into enormous industrial centers, the world population was a lot smaller and technological innovations that were to reshape the world were still on the drawing board.

Since technology had not yet taken a foothold, we depended more on other people to meet our economic and social needs. Not so today, however. We live in a vast technological arena where the communication process is so complex, many of us are not quite sure where to turn for information. We're bombarded by sights, sounds, words and pictures. With all this in the foreground, it's easy to make a case for public relations.

Communication Skills

If one word could sum up what public relations work is all about, it is *communication*. Robert Marston, of Robert Marston & Associates in New York, defines it this way: "Public relations is planned, persuasive communication designed to influence significant publics."

A seasoned public relations worker prides himself on being able to exchange information in clear-cut, easily understandable terms. What separates the pros from the rank amateurs? Simple—their ability and skill in communication.

For now, we're using the word communicate in its broadest sense. Later on, we'll fine-tune it to the many different public relations instruments commonly used—news releases, speeches, press conferences, etc.

Occasionally, you'll stumble on a Renaissance-type public relations worker who can communicate effectively on a number of fronts. More typically, public relations workers specialize in a particular area, depending upon their expertise. If you're the outgoing type, you might enjoy spending the major part of your time working with clients or prospective clients and members of the media. Public relations account executives, as they are called, are at their best when they're shaking people's hands and presenting their client's story over lunch or cocktails. Needless to say, to be a first-rate account executive, you have to enjoy and be good at close person-to-person contact. This is how account executives communicate best. Instead of putting their client's or company's story down on paper, they're more effective when they're talking about it.

On the other hand, a public relations writer is often referred to as a desk person, since the better part of the day is spent in the office as opposed to the field. Instead of talking, the communication medium is the written word. This is also true for the public relations speech writer, whose primary function is to research and write speeches for a company's or client's top brass.

And while most public relations workers specialize in a particular facet of PR work, many public relations agency owners have, at different points in their careers, worked in a variety of capacities, from writing releases and speeches and contacting clients to engineering lavish promotional campaigns. Having worked in all the key areas, they are better equipped to delegate authority and assign work to those who are knowledgeable enough to carry it out.

External Versus Internal Communication

There are two broad types of communication used by PR workers: external communication and internal communication.

Let's start with external communication and go back to the International Widget Company for a moment as it prepares to market its new line of super widgets. When the curtain abruptly came down, company employees were in a frenzy, its high-ranking executives could barely get to sleep at night and the overworked public relations staff was not about to take a normal breath until the new widget was introduced to the public in grand style.

The PR staff's primary goal is to reach the public in the most effective manner possible. This is an example of external communication in action. The PR staff strives to "break the product" and get maximum publicity. This might mean anything and everything from securing media exposure (television, radio and print) to planning lavish direct-mail programs to prospective widget users.

But once the new product is introduced, the company's PR staff might be involved with the internal communication process. Internal communication refers to public relations functions that are concentrated within the organization itself. A highly functional corporation like International Widget, for example, realizes the importance of creating a comfortable working environment for its employees. Over the past couple of years the company has given its employees a number of fringe benefits, such as a longer afternoon coffee break, a small gymnasium where employees can exercise during their lunch hour or after work and reduced airfare to certain vacation resorts.

All of the programs were introduced by the public relations department and they are only a few of the successful ways of establishing open internal communication between management and employees.

Many large companies distribute internal house organs, or company publications, to their employees. We'll spend more time on house organs later on, but for now it's important to know that it's another internal communication avenue commonly used by PR departments.

Or if management wishes to announce a new program or company-sponsored courses that employees can avail themselves of in order to better their position within the company, the program will probably be introduced by the public relations department. This is another example of internal communication.

Within large companies it's quite common for large public relations staffs to be loosely carved into internal and external workers. One worker, for example, might edit the company newsletter, which involves maintaining close and productive working relationships with employees. He or she might prepare stories about enterprising workers who are moving up through the ranks, report on marriages, births and deaths, and also be a sounding board for employee grievances.

Public relations workers involved in external public relations concentrate all of their efforts on keeping their company's name before the media. Keep in mind, however, that in most small-to-medium-sized companies, PR workers are jacks-of-all-trades, performing both internal and external functions.

Creative Intermediaries

In the process of communicating either internally or externally, public relations workers function as creative intermediaries. If you're involved in external communication, for example, your job is to act as a buffer between the company and the outside world. When someone requests information about your company, be it a reporter on a trade paper or a customer, you are the company representative or spokesperson. You speak for the company and are responsible for getting the company's message across.

If a member of the press requests an interview with the president of your company, you are the one who makes all the arrangements. If the reporter wants to know about a discontinued product or information about next year's earnings projection, this too falls into your domain. Many of the routine questions can be answered without doing any research. But if you don't have the answers handy, you're responsible for getting them as promptly as possible.

A public relations worker's job has its tense moments also. If the company is in trouble, be it a legal dispute or a barrage of customer complaints, you're the one who will have to face the cameras and microphones and defend your company to the media.

If a company is embroiled in a heavily publicized lawsuit, rarely do you find the company's president on the six o'clock news. More likely, a company spokesperson, which is a fancy title for public

8

relations representative, is before the camera, coolly and professionally fielding questions. In cases like this, the director of public relations sits down with the company's president and between them they decide upon a strategy for handling the problem.

Or, if most of your job responsibilities revolve around formulating internal public relations strategies, you might have to act as the intermediary between management and employees.

From whatever angle you look at it, as a public relations worker you'll be functioning as a middle person, whether it be between management and employees, management and the press, or the company and its customers. You have an important job. After all, you *are* the voice or instrument that dispenses up-to-the-minute information about your product, company, agency or client.

Presenting the Right Image

In acting as a creative intermediary or liaison, your job is to present your client in the best possible light. You've probably read or heard a great deal about corporate or product images. A good part of a public relations worker's time is spent in creating a true and undistorted image of what a company, or product, is all about. This isn't always easy, especially if you're talking about a gigantic multinational conglomerate whose products are competing in an international marketplace.

For example, imagine that you're the head of a national drug company and you've just introduced a new and controversial toothpaste that is supposed to reduce tooth decay by 20 percent. Naturally, your competition has no intention of letting you capture the marketplace. No sooner does your new toothpaste hit the market than an anticipated product war begins. Your leading competitor wastes no time telling the consumer press that your product is a gigantic rip-off and cannot, in fact, reduce tooth decay. With one sweeping statement, your credibility has been questioned. What do you do?

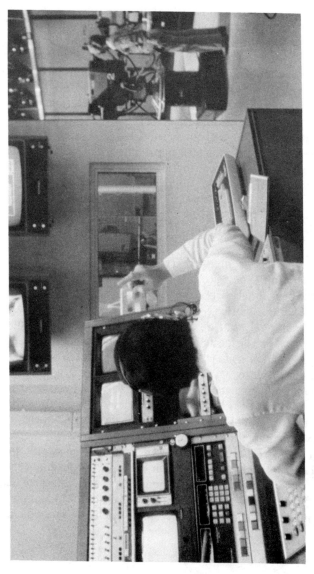

3M's public relations department includes audio/visual communications services that provide photography, video presentations, scripts and other professional services. Videotapes of products are used in electronic media, as well as to aid editors of print media. (Photo courtesy of Minnesota Mining and Manufacturing)

What Is Public Relations?

The first thing that has to be done is to schedule a long meeting with your PR director in order to fashion a counter strategy that will right the tables and present the true story to the public. This might include drawing upon medical evidence that states your toothpaste actually reduces tooth decay. Your goal is to restore the company's good image and leave no doubt in anyone's mind that your company is reliable, honest and truthful, and, most important, that your product does what it says it can do. To drive home these important points, your public relations staff will stand on their collective head to present the company in the most favorable light.

A poor image can be disastrous and a strained one can have a negative effect on sales over the long term. So it's not hard to understand why a PR worker will bend over backwards to get the right image across.

Celebrities, for example, retain public relations firms to make sure that the public sees the image they want to project. Often you'll read about a heated controversy in the press over what a reporter views as the projected image and what he thinks the true image is all about. If it's a big star whose name is constantly making headlines, it often makes for sizzling copy. This is another form of public relations work. There are public relations firms that work exclusively with celebrities. Their job is to secure favorable publicity and exposure for their clients. It might mean wining and dining members of the entertainment press in order to secure favorable interviews and reviews.

A public relations firm that represents a rock and roll star will burn the midnight oil to come up with a promotional strategy that creates a saleable image for the client. Just any image won't do. It has to be one that captivates and snares the band's projected audience.

Imagine that the Conrad Celebrity Ltd., a public relations firm that specializes in promoting musical acts, just took on a new client —a wildly talented teenage rock and roll band that hopes to make it big with the early teen set.

Conrad has a tough job ahead of them. Out of the vast music-buying public they have the difficult job of exciting the imaginations of teen listeners.

After countless, tiresome meetings, Conrad's PR executives and the band's manager and agent devise a strategy that they hope will launch the band in grand style.

The next step is targeting key members of the rock and national press who are likely to give the band favorable publicity. Once that is taken care of, press packets are mailed out. The packet includes a press release announcing the new band and its forthcoming album, several pictures of the band and an invitation to a press party to hear and meet them and enjoy drinks and a buffet supper. As reporters and media representatives arrive at the party they will be greeted by a smiling public relations worker, who will hand them the band's new album, plus more press material.

This is only Conrad Celebrity's opening strategy for introducing the band. Knowing how competitive the market is, they've further outlined a five-part campaign spread over six months to draw attention to the band. Even then, there is no guarantee that they will succeed. If they manage to create a favorable image, and garner a favorable response from the media, they stand to keep their clients and possibly gain other emerging groups as well. And if they fail, they have to go back to the drawing board and analyze their press campaigns to try to find out what went wrong.

So whether it's a product, band, comedian, actor or actress, public relations workers go to great lengths to create an image that will sell their client or product to the public.

Many Different Applications

Now you can better understand how public relations is used as a multipurpose tool. Within a large company it can be used to strengthen the communication lines between management and employees. In a nonprofit organization, public relations helps bring the organization's goals and objectives before the public. If it's a corporation selling a product, public relations techniques are used as auxiliary selling tools. And governments—federal, state, and local—use public relations to acquaint the public with new programs, laws and issues. That's only a brief sampling of public relations in action.

As you can see, public relations is a large field whose techniques, strategies and applications can be used to benefit many different types of organizations. Later on, we'll go into more detail about some of the exciting public relations fields you might want to explore.

What It Is Not

The first mistake people make is thinking advertising and public relations are the same thing. While public relations and advertising programs are often closely related, their goals are different.

Typically, advertising has a more pressing sales objective. Advertisers pay a great deal of money for space and time. It can cost an advertiser thousands of dollars for a single page in a magazine or newspaper. Depending upon the type of magazine, its audience and popularity, the cost of advertising space can vary considerably. It's quite common to pay as much as $30,000 for a single color page. And that's considered a meager sum compared to what television time costs. A 15-second TV ad delivered in prime time can cost a lot more. Since advertising time and space are so expensive, companies try to get their messages across in the most effective and penetrating ways possible. For that brief period—as long as it takes 15 or 30 seconds to race by or the time it takes to scan a full- or half-page ad in a magazine—the advertiser has the challenging job of capturing the consumers and holding their attention. If a considerable number of potential customers are not reached, time and money are wasted.

Public relations, on the other hand, attempts to influence people, and possibly stimulate sales as well, over a longer time period. Public relations workers don't have to resort to sledgehammer tactics to get their points across. They're not restricted to seconds and

13

outrageous prices for advertising time and space. Their goal is to make a lasting impact, to hold a listener's or reader's attention for a longer time period.

Yet within many large companies, advertising and public relations departments work closely in formulating sales strategies. Between the two departments, they develop strategies that cover the near and long term. The techniques used by the two departments, although different in approach, complement each other nicely. After all, their ultimate goals are the same.

On the other hand, a company that has developed a tasteless and misleading advertising program is not going to enjoy favorable public relations. The public relations department is placed in the embarrassing position of defending allegations from consumers and manufacturers, not to mention legal hassles. However, if a company's advertising is professional, honest and tasteful, it is safe to conclude that the company will also enjoy excellent public relations.

Another common stereotype is thinking public relations workers spend their time wining and dining clients, shaking hands and being pleasant. If that's all public relations work consisted of, public relations firms and large companies could save an enormous amount of money in salaries to speech writers and account executives, and purchase smiling, handshaking robots to do the job instead. Being pleasant, taking clients out to dinner and arranging parties is certainly a part of a public relations worker's job. But it only amounts to a fractional part of the job. There will be a great deal more on this topic in Chapter Two, when we describe the many different skills used by PR representatives.

Why Public Relations Is Important

By now you should have a better idea of what public relations work is all about. At its best, it can be compared to a free-flowing stream where ideas and information pass unimpeded from one source to another. If it's internal public relations, information flows from management to employees, allowing greater understanding and cooperation. If it's external public relations, information flows from the organization to the public, achieving a desired or planned goal.

As we mentioned earlier, instant communication is no longer difficult to achieve. Within moments, you can talk to the farthest point on the globe. Yet a century ago, the communication process took a great deal longer. At that time the world wasn't encircled by a sophisticated communication web connecting every town and city on the globe.

Today, efficient and direct communication is essential. Not only do governments need and depend upon public relations, but so do organizations of every kind, from the small, growing business to the multinational conglomerate. Once you can appreciate how important public relations is in our modern world, you'll understand why words like *influence, persuade, convince* and *attention* all fit into a global definition of what public relations is all about.

We've only touched the surface. Now let's take a look at some of the key public relations functions.

2

Public Relations Serves Many Functions

Depending upon the type of organization you're working for, public relations can mean many different things. If you're a public relations representative employed by a small, prestigious engineering school, you have your own special problems, frustrations and challenges. Or if you're the public relations worker employed by a large PR agency, and your job is to outline a multimillion-dollar public relations campaign for a large tire company, you're probably up to your ears in pressure from your employer and client to get the project done a certain way.

No matter what type of public relations work you're involved in, you can expect challenges that are unique to that project. But no matter what sector of the business you work in, there are basic functions that can be attributed to all public relations work. Let's take a look at some of them.

Programming and Policy Formation

Imagine a small, family-operated business that owns two medium-sized supermarkets. It's a well-established, growing business employing over 100 employees. As expected, the executive positions are filled by family members and the rest are outsiders—managers, clerks, stock and delivery people and cashiers. Next year, if profits are sizable, the family plans to open another supermarket, further expanding its operating base. For the time being, however, the business is run smoothly with no major organizational problems. The communication lines are simple and direct. Since top management is accessible, workers can go right to the top if they have any problems without having to contend with middle management. Missing is a complicated chain of command.

If an employee has a complaint, he doesn't have to go through a personnel or public relations department. All he has to do is knock on the boss's door and if he's not busy on the phone or negotiating with a salesperson, he'll resolve the employee's difficulty right then and there. Not so with a large sprawling corporation employing thousands of employees.

Employees of an electric utility company, for example, can't stroll into the president's office every time they have a problem. It's more complicated. If an employee has a complaint, the first thing he has to do is find out who to complain to. Typically, the chain of command is long and it could take weeks before something is done about the problem. You can appreciate why so many people fear getting lost within a large corporation.

Our fictional utility may have over 2,000 people working in one large facility, compared with 100 workers employed by the family-owned supermarket. The larger the organization, the more rules and regulations are needed to run it. If they didn't exist, you'd have chaos and disorganization.

The average worker employed by a large corporation rarely has anything to do with the president of the company. He might go through as many as ten different job promotions and salary changes and still never see the chief operating officer. The promotions are swiftly and efficiently administered by the company's executive corps. And rules concerning promotions, vacations, sick leave, pension plans and general corporate policy are planned, published and explained by the company's public relations department.

Don't forget, our giant utility is a far cry from the small family-owned-and-operated supermarket. The supermarket has minor organizational problems compared to the massive public utility. Since the business is small, promotion from clerk to assistant manager to manager is simple and direct. Yet within the utility, ascending the corporate ladder from maintenance person to first-line supervisor is complicated, involving a number of promotions and salary changes. The more jobs, skills and people you have in an organization, the more it takes to control and manage it.

Employee Relations

Within large corporations, public relations workers plan and coordinate programs concerning all matters that affect employees, ranging from grievance outlets and promotional policies to in-house educational and training facilities for workers who hope to be promoted to better jobs.

Let's take a look at what some of your job responsibilities would be if you worked for the public relations department of an international computer manufacturer. You're part of a 25-person public relations staff and, like most competent PR workers, your responsibilities vary from day to day.

On a typical day, you might be coordinating five different projects at the same time. Your first meeting is a breakfast budget meeting at 8:15 with the president and the top officers of the company. The purpose of the meeting is to decide how much of the yearly budget is going to be allocated for employee relations. Last year's budget calculations have to be revised in the light of new objectives, better programs, a more functional communication network between employees and management. Up until now, the relationship between management and workers has only been satisfactory. But as a result of union pressures and complaints from employees who have been with the firm a long time, management feels that more funds have to be set aside for employee relations.

For over three hours information is exchanged between the executives. The head of the public relations department makes a good argument in favor of a new lounge and gymnasium for employees. While it will cost over $30,000 to take an unused room and make it into a gym, he feels it will signifcantly boost employee morale. He argues that more and more companies are spending money on inhouse recreational facilities for their employees, ranging from fully equipped gymnasiums to indoor tracks. He asks his fellow executives not to be shortsighted, to see beyond the initial investment to the long-range returns. A happy worker, he explains, will be more productive, and will be more likely to give 100 percent of himself to his work.

At the end of the lengthy session, the majority of executives, including the president, agree with their PR director, and plans are made to get firm estimates on the cost of building the gymnasium. The PR director is asked to get comparative costs for the building of the gym along with projections on how long the project will take from start to finish.

Employee Advancement Programs

After a quick lunch, our overworked PR director attends another meeting, this time with lower-level management. The purpose of the meeting is to improve advancement opportunities for company workers. Through a union grievance committee, management learned that many workers are frustrated and dissatisfied because of all the red tape involved in advancing from one job slot to another. Management has been aware of the problem for some time, but up until now, has done nothing about it. Now that complaints are coming in fast and furiously from workers, however, management has decided to do something about the problem immediately. And to make matters more urgent, it has come to the attention of top management, via the company's vice-president of personnel, that a small yet significant percentage of workers are leaving each year to take better jobs with other companies.

Once the problem is identified, the burden of responsibility to improve advancement opportunities for nonmanagement employees is placed on the PR director's shoulders. And it's not a simple problem by any means. Before our harried PR director can even think about developing a program and strategy to right the situation, he needs time to formulate a course of action.

Two days after his meeting with top management, he calls an impromptu meeting with five senior members of his staff to talk about the problem and outline a plan.

After lengthy discussions, the PR staff concludes the problem is one of ineffective and poor communication lines between management and employees. Advancement opportunities exist. The problem, however, is that employees are not aware of them. And if they do hear about an opening, they're not sure how to go about qualifying for it.

Over a four-day period, the public relations staff maps out a plan calling for the publication of bulletins informing employees of job openings and how to qualify for them. To give it priority, they decide to publish a special eight-page edition of the company newsletter, telling employees about advancement opportunities and preparatory company-sponsored courses. Again, the goal of the public relations department is to improve employee relations and to open up the communication lines so information can flow freely from management to employees and vice versa.

Scheduling Budget Conferences

Our busy public relations department also has the yearly chore of scheduling budget conferences with the company's regional managers. The PR department has to be concerned with the total functioning of the company. It would be simple if all they had to do was coordinate activities within the corporation's main office. However, the company maintains 25 regional offices throughout the United States and the PR department has to keep in touch with all of them. To keep abreast of regional happenings and to revise budgets for the next year, the company schedules yearly budget conferences with regional heads and the senior executive staff.

The job of planning the conferences and making all the necessary arrangements falls into the public relations department's lap. The first thing the PR staff has to do is decide on a convenient time period when everyone can attend. Once a time is established, all the necessary arrangements can be made. Transportation is arranged and hotel rooms are reserved months in advance. And finally, conferences have to be scheduled over a three-day period, giving the executive corps enough time to accomplish everything that has to be done.

Once this event is successfully completed, chances are there is another important conference or meeting six months down the road that has to be scheduled, planned and coordinated.

Relationships

As you can see, the public relations department of a large corporation occupies a pivotal position. At some point it is involved with all facets of the corporation. In order to achieve effective public relations, PR representatives have to maintain a good working relationship with all departments within the company. In the process of creating a productive relationship, PR workers are concerned with improving *upward* and *downward* communication.

Downward communication refers to the communication lines between management and employees. Management uses a variety of methods to keep the communication lines open so information flows freely. Vehicles of downward communication include employee magazines, newspapers, newsletters, bulletin boards, films, announcement posters, reading racks, letters, ceremonies and interoffice memorandums.

Typically, the upward communication lines are not as well developed and more often than not present a challenge for public relations staffs. Vehicles of upward communication are usually suggestion or complaint boxes and open group meetings where employees can express opinions and make their needs known.

As a company expands, the public relations department is faced with the challenge of formulating workable upward communication lines so employees are in a better position to improve their positions within the company. With tight and functional upward communication lines management can better deal with problems as they occur, instead of waiting until a crisis arises.

Public relations workers who work exclusively with internal public relations and maintain free-flowing downward and upward communication lines have a full-time job. To appreciate how complications can arise, imagine gathering 100 people in one room and asking each person the same question. What kinds of answers do you think you'll get? There's a good chance you'll get 100 different answers. So you can appreciate the challenges facing PR workers who devote most of their time to internal public relations.

A public relations worker's relationships extend far beyond the company's home office, where the executive staff manages and directs the company's operations. Often, a PR worker will travel to a distant regional office to gather information, or merely as a goodwill trip to make sure everything is functioning as it should.

To sum up, as management representatives, public relations workers try to maintain good working relationships with the entire staff, whether they be management or unskilled workers on an assembly line. A public relations worker's responsibilities extend to all employees, regardless of rank, status and salary level.

Writing, Editing, Interviewing

One of the most effective tools public relations workers have at their disposal is the printed word. Depending upon the public relations department, its strategy, goals and long-term objectives, the printed word is used in any number of ways.

Large public relations departments have editorial staffs consisting of writers, editors and production people. Depending upon the particular project, a PR writer might help put together a company newsletter, magazine or newspaper; write articles for trade magazines, prepare speeches and news releases and supervise the preparation of quarterly and annual reports. Rarely do you find PR writers who are involved in all of the above. However, it's safe to say that your average PR writer will be involved in a number of writing projects.

Press Releases

The press release is a basic tool used by public relations writers to gain media coverage. It is a tightly written one- or two-page statement describing an event, news item, product, appointment, or TV or radio promotion. The idea behind the release is to arouse the reader's attention.

Press releases are sent to newspapers, trade magazines and to television and radio stations. When you consider the number of different organizations, businesses and PR agencies that routinely prepare press releases, it's not hard to understand how a press release can be prepared on wide-ranging subjects. Regardless of the subject, however, the purpose of the release is to gain *immediate attention.*

The best releases are brief. Nevertheless, a lot of time is spent preparing them. A release is written so that its reader can absorb the material quickly without having to go back and read it twice. They're simply written, direct and to the point. In fact, the best of them appear to be deceptively simple. Don't be fooled, however. It's quite common for an experienced public relations writer to spend a couple of hours writing one release consisting of a little over 200 words. The real challenge is preparing a straightforward release based on weighty, technical material.

An experienced public relations writer knows when a release is accomplishing its goal. If you send a press release to a newspaper or magazine and you don't hear from them, or eventually see anything in print, it's safe to assume your release wound up in the wastepaper basket unread. All too often releases are discarded because they're poorly written, so unclear that the editor can't be bothered deciphering the essence of the story.

This is why public relations writers agonize over the preparation of a single release. If it's about an important event, the release of a new product—such as the announcement of the debut date of the super widget mentioned in the introduction—a great deal of time is invested in preparing a crystal-clear, succinctly written release.

The best a public relations worker can hope for from a press release is a call from an editor inquiring about doing a feature story based upon the material in the release. And even if the material in the release is reduced to three or four lines in a trade magazine or newspaper, the public relations writer has accomplished his goal, drawing attention to his client, project or news item.

In large public relations agencies it's quite common for releases to be rewritten a number of times before they're printed and mailed out. A junior PR writer usually does the first draft before it is turned over to a senior writer for another rewrite. Finally, the reworked copy winds up on a supervising editor's desk where more changes are made.

When the junior writer finally sees his release in its finished form, he's startled to learn that the final copy is radically different from what he wrote. The lead might be shorter and more to the point, and the essence of the story may have been reduced from 500 words to a tight 250 words. Put yourself in the junior writer's shoes, if you can. You would probably be understandably upset when you discover that the final version of the release barely resembles the copy you presented. Yet, this is par for the course and an important part of the process whereby junior writers learn to hone their skills before they advance to the position of senior writer. If you're serious about mastering your craft, you'll learn to put your ego aside and profit from your mistakes.

Take a look at the enclosed sample releases. If you were working on this account, would you make any changes in the releases or leave them as they are?

Sample Press Release

From: Brightline, Inc.
3387 Avenue of the Americas
New York, N.Y. 10036

FOR IMMEDIATE RELEASE

NEW MULTICOLOR PLASTIC WINDOW DISPLAY SIGNS
BY BRIGHTLINE PROVIDE EYE-CATCHING
PRODUCT PROMOTIONS

New York, N.Y.—Multicolor plastic window display signs that turn an ordinary store window into an eye-catching product preview are announced by Brightline, Inc., a leader in the design and manufacturing of flexible packaging.

Plastic window display signs by Brightline offer a user distinct advantages over paper window display signs. The colors on Brightline signs are more durable and have a longer useful life than paper signs. They are reusable, simple to put up and take down and adhere to all flat surfaces without the need for taping of any sort. Another significant advantage of plastic window signs is that they do not cut off outside light as paper signs do. Outside light filters through the plastic to provide light for the interior of the store.

Brightline offers a customer an integrated service from conception, design, manufacturing, printing, to delivery. Brightline plastic window display signs are also made in transparent polyethylene, which provides for even greater penetration of light into a store.

For information on Brightline window display signs, write: Brightline, Inc., 3387 Avenue of the Americas, New York, N.Y. 10036.

Sample Press Release

From: Brightline, Inc.
3387 Avenue of the Americas
New York, N.Y. 10036

FOR IMMEDIATE RELEASE

BRIGHTLINE BRINGS THE EXCITEMENT
OF POSTERIZATION TO PLASTIC BAGS

New York, N.Y.—Brightline, Inc. has developed a process which permits the sweep and excitement of posterization to be brought to plastic tote bags. The graphic variations possible with posterization make the process a valuable tool for premium, promotional and advertising programs. Posterization simulates multicolor dramatic effects. It permits an almost infinite variety of these effects to be obtained through full-color printing.

Posterization can be seen on the wide variety of Brightline plastic tote bags which will be on display at the 54th Annual Premium Show, May 10-19, at the New York Coliseum, booths 2310 and 2311.

Brightline plastic tote bags provide premiums that are vividly different, dramatically bold and have extremely high visibility. For further information about how posterization and Brightline plastic carrier and shopping bags can work for you as a premium, contact: Brightline, Inc., 3387 Avenue of the Americas, New York, N.Y. 10036.

House Organs

A house organ is an all-inclusive term covering a variety of company publications that represent a vital form of internal communication. It could be a four-, six- or eight-page newsletter, a company newspaper and even a slick four-color magazine, the kind you see on your neighborhood newsstand. These all fall into the loose category of house organs. They're produced by a company's public relations department and are distributed to all employees. The rule of thumb is the larger the company, the bigger and more expensive the house organ. International Business Machines (IBM), General Motors and Bausch & Lomb, for example, have expensive four-color magazines that are as impressive as any magazine you'll see on a newsstand. But whether it's a fancy 64-page monthly magazine or a quarterly mimeographed eight-page newsletter, they all serve a similar purpose. They keep employees informed of current happenings within the company such as births, deaths, and promotions, as well as news items and world developments. And if it's an international company, workers can read about how their fellow workers are faring abroad. Company magazines routinely profile workers, giving readers a glimpse of what it's like living and working in another state or, perhaps, another country.

Executives in one part of the country get a chance to find out what fellow executives are doing and how they worked their way up the corporate ladder. All in all, house organs, especially those prepared by the PR departments of sprawling multinational companies, bring employees closer together.

Production

Public relations workers are not directly involved with the actual production of company newsletters, magazines or newspapers. Yet, they are expected to know something about layout, typography and photography in order to supervise the production of them. In producing a company newsletter, for example, the public relations staff works closely with the production staff.

Setting up a visual display designed to enhance a corporate image is a vital skill in public relations. (Photo courtesy of Real World Photos)

As editor of your company's in-house publication, you have some definite ideas on how the stories should be laid out. First, you want the stories presented in a certain order and then you want them to make an attractive graphic presentation. In order to accomplish this, you have to know something about type styles, cropping and sizing photos so they fit precisely to your page, and something about preparing headlines that attract attention. Or if a layout for a story or photo spread is not exciting enough, you have to be able to guide the art director so that it is redone to your specifications.

In short, you have to be familiar with every aspect of the publication, from conception of article ideas, production and layout to the actual printing of it. After all, it's your product and you want it to be as perfect as it can possibly be.

Annual and Quarterly Reports

Many public relations writers specialize in preparing quarterly and annual reports. It's not uncommon to find generalist PR writers doing this along with other writing functions. But since it is technical writing, it requires not only good writing skills, but a financial or business background as well. The public relations writer works closely with the company's president or comptroller in reviewing the company's financial record for the past year, along with looking ahead to new developments (new products, increased earnings, changes in staff) in the upcoming calendar or fiscal year.

The quarterly and annual reports are vitally important because they provide an accurate summation of how well the company is doing and what its plans are for the future. And since they're read by potential and current investors, the media and members of the financial community, they must be professionally prepared, informative and well-written. A great deal of care is given to putting these reports together so that they reap positive results. To insure accuracy they're usually sent to the company's attorneys and accountants before they're approved for printing.

Speech Writing

Speech writing is another highly skilled type of public relations writing. What with hectic schedules, high-ranking corporate executives and politicians, for example, hardly have time to sit down and write their own speeches. Instead, they depend upon members of the public relations staff to write the speeches for them. Compared to other types of public relations writing, only a small number specialize in this field, which explains why speech writers are always in demand and why they're well paid for their efforts.

Speech writing requires a different type of writing talent. You might not be aware of it, but we don't write and speak the same way. The challenge for the speech writer is capturing the other person's speech patterns and speaking style. A successful speech has to be informative, interesting and, when possible, humorous.

Information

An experienced public relations representative prides himself on 'his information sources. Once you know how information can be used to best advantage, you then have to have outlets for the information. A junior public relations worker can expect to spend a couple of years developing information sources and contacts. He quickly learns that preparing and gathering the information is only the first step. The next step is putting that information to work.

Let's go back to the harried public relations workers at International Widget. In the process of getting ready to launch the super widget, the PR staff outlined a media strategy. First, releases and product sheets describing the new widget were written. While this was being done a list of key media people at newspapers, trade magazines, and radio and TV stations was prepared. Names were picked carefully. They were contacts who were most likely to read the material and give it publicity.

You can have the greatest story in the world but if you don't have an outlet for it, or vehicle for telling the world about it, it's useless.

Public Relations Serves Many Functions

No matter what aspect of public relations work you're involved in, you have to be very creative when it comes to finding the right information sources that can do the most good.

An exciting aspect of public relations work is that there is no patented way of gaining publicity for a product or client. There are many options open to a PR worker, and it's up to you to find the most effective communication channel.

A skilled public relations representative can often get immediate exposure for his client or product by merely making a single telephone call. Let's say your client developed a new flashlight that has unlimited life and, if properly promoted, could revolutionize the entire flashlight industry. Prior to sending out press releases to all the appropriate media channels, you call an old friend who happens to be editor in chief of one of the most influential national electronics trade magazines. Instead of telling him about the exciting new product over the telephone, you suggest meeting for lunch to discuss an exciting story that might interest him. Naturally the editor is curious and agrees to meet you for lunch.

Over a two-hour lunch, you carefully and diplomatically outline the story and its ultimate effect on the electronics industry. As expected, the editor's curiosity is aroused. While you describe the new product, he busily takes notes and asks questions. Convinced that it is a first-rate story and thankful for the exclusive, he promises to give the story a full page in the next issue of the magazine.

Being an experienced PR representative, you knew exactly what you were doing. You knew the editor would jump at the story and would appreciate an exclusive. So a leisurely two-hour lunch paid off handsomely.

As you can see, PR workers understand the media. They realize that the heart and soul of any publication, whether it be consumer or trade, is reliable, new and interesting stories. Magazines and newspapers will go out of their way to get their hands on that special story no one else has — an interview with a famous person who has never granted an interview, or news of a product or drug that will have a major impact on an industry. Public relations workers are aware of this and know which media outlet will deliver the best results. And equally important, they know whom to call to get the fastest possible results.

A seasoned public relations worker has a battery of information sources he carries from job to job. Very often your contacts and information sources can be crucial in determining whether you qualify for a job. If you're applying for a position as a PR writer with a chemical company, for instance, and you have a number of important chemical industry contacts, your chances of getting the job are a lot better than if you had no contacts at all.

Aside from having contacts and information sources, you also have to know how the media works, and how long it takes to get information to the public. For example, a daily newspaper can release a story within 24 hours after receiving it, whereas monthly magazines work with a 90-day lead time. By the time a story is published, it's already old news. It's dated and no one cares. As a hardworking PR worker, you're faced with the challenge of finding the most appropriate media avenue.

Along with skillfully handling information, public relations workers are often involved with coordinating and arranging special events. This could be anything from a press conference, dinner, tour or demonstration to a parade.

Let's say you work for a large automaker that just automated 25 percent of its assembly line with robots — a big event warranting publicity. Working closely with the executive staff, you arrange to invite key media representatives to the plant for a guided tour and demonstration of the facility by the company's chief product engineer.

Your goal is to publicize the event, informing the public that your company is using the latest in advanced technology to produce efficient and cost-effective automobiles.

Or, if your company is scheduled to attend a convention, you'll be responsible for setting up a booth where your company's products will be on display. Again, planning and coordination are necessary. Prior to the event, you'll have to arrange for delivery of the products to the convention site, along with appropriate back-up literature. And at the convention, you'll have to meet with members of the press in order to tell them about new product developments and plans for the upcoming year.

In coordinating special events, you'll have to plan on doing some traveling. The extent of your traveling in any given year will largely depend upon your responsibilities and the type of company you represent. If you're the public relations director of an international conglomerate that sells its products around the world, it's safe to assume you'll be doing quite a bit of traveling. If a new plant opens or a new product is developed by one of your subsidiary companies, or you're arranging for the president of the company to visit all of the North American subsidiaries, you'll be expected to make all the necessary arrangements and see that everything proceeds on schedule.

Speaking

As a representative of your company, you might have to speak in your company's behalf, give lectures about your company's products and future developments, or single-handedly conduct press conferences. These job responsibilities are reserved for senior members of the public relations staff and most likely it's the PR director who actually speaks for his company.

If you were a junior member of a PR staff, for example, you might be expected to introduce key members of your staff to the media, or possibly introduce the president of your company to the press. Later on, when you're more experienced, you'll be called upon to actually represent your company.

It's not uncommon for public relations workers to give lectures to company employees concerning new products or explain company policies, and even to be a guest lecturer at a college or university.

Experienced public relations workers often have to make informal presentations as well as give formal speeches. After working in the field for a number of years, they have mastered all aspects of the communication process. They're comfortable with people and

There are a number of ways to approach PR . . . by phone and by doing your homework in a company library. (Photo courtesy of Vista)

language, and they can just as easily write informative news releases as make an impromptu speech if they have to. Face-to-face communication doesn't faze them in the least.

Research and Evaluation

Whether you're involved in programming, preparing a house organ, gathering information, writing speeches or making arrangements for a demonstration and lecture tour, research and fact-gathering are a crucial part of the PR worker's job.

A PR representative often has to spend hours gathering information and poring over facts, figures and statistics in order to prepare detailed, accurate and timely material.

Imagine that you work for a company that dominates the soft lens market. You're part of a 15-person public relations staff. You have to prepare a press release about the company's newest and most revolutionary soft lens that is just about to be introduced to the public.

It sounds simple enough, yet there is more to it than you think. Just having all the information on the new lens is only the first step. It is certainly valuable, but that's not the whole story. What you don't know is how extensive the soft lens market is. Who has done what? What is the competition like? Why is your company's new soft lens so special?

You may never actually use all the information you gather, but as a spokesperson and expert on your company's products, you have to know your product from stem to stern. You have to know its advantages and shortcomings (if any), and you have to be able to discuss them intelligently within the context of the current market environment.

In gathering the information, you'll probably have to spend a few hours in the library poring over past and current developments in the field, and possibly speak to a few experts for a technical perspective.

Or suppose your client is an emerging actor your public relations agency feels is a potential star. The agency, which happens to specialize in public relations for actors, singers and musicians, is currently in the process of preparing a press kit for the actor. The press kit will include a couple of eight by ten photographs (called glossies), along with a four-page biography (bio). The production staff is in charge of the photos, while you're responsible for writing the bio.

The bio is a valuable media tool. Magazine and newspaper writers use them as source material to prepare stories and reviews. A biography contains all the blood and guts information a writer needs to write a factual story: age, background, credentials, insights and pertinent quotes from the entertainer that can enliven a story.

The first thing you'll do is interview the actor at great length. Equipped with a pen, pencil or tape recorder, you'll try to get as much information as you can. By spending time with your client, you'll try to get a sense of what the person is all about. Instead of delivering dry facts, you are going to whet an editor's appetite by highlighting interesting facts and observations about this person. Possibly, he did some unconventional things in order to gain recognition, or he might have faced a great deal of opposition in his climb to the top.

Once you've gathered all the facts, you'll go back to your office and prepare a first draft of the bio. Based upon the material you've gathered, you'll be able to produce an informative biography that will help the young actor get the publicity he needs.

Or, if you're in the midst of preparing your company's annual report, chances are you'll spend a lot of time with your company's attorneys and accountants gathering information for the report. You'll also be talking to regional managers to find out if there are any significant developments that warrant mentioning.

In preparing speeches, speech writers practically live with the person for whom they are preparing the speech. Aside from gathering the information, they also have to know something about how the person thinks, talks and expresses himself. If he has a unique way of turning a phrase, for example, the speech writer will try to capture that facet of his personality when writing the speech.

No matter what the project or assignment, it will undoubtedly involve a certain amount of research, fact-gathering and evaluation. The public relations representative has the challenging and often difficult job of accurately presenting his client to the public. To accomplish that end, it often requires days, weeks and, sometimes, months of research.

As you can see, PR workers wear many hats. They perform many different functions, each of which is nearly a profession in itself.

3

Public Relations Fields

All of the functions mentioned in the preceding chapter are used at one time or another by the different organizations and businesses that depend upon public relations. Each organization has different needs and goals, and the public relations worker faces the challenge of adapting public relations principles and tactics to the organization he serves.

Corporate Public Relations

The majority of public relations workers are employed by corporations. Depending upon the size of the company and the industry it serves, the public relations staff could be anything from a one-person department to an entire in-house facility the size of a public relations agency.

As we said earlier, every company is different. Beyond size, each caters to a separate market and produces different products and services. The public relations tactics for an international oil company are far different from those used by a clothing manufacturer, supply company or recording company. While the businesses and products differ, public relations fundamentals and practices remain the same. It's just a question of adapting those principles and prac-

Press conferences are a big part of the public relations person's work. And they are sometimes difficult to run properly. (Photo courtesy of Real World Photos)

tices to the needs of the industry or company you're working for. Let's take a look at some of the different types of businesses that rely on public relations.

Large Versus Small Retailers

A large urban department store, for example, requires both internal and external public relations. Both are vitally important to insure continued growth. Good internal public relations are necessary because the store's personnel work closely with customers and it's important that a good working rapport exist at all times. The PR staff of a large, centrally located urban store works hard to insure an open communication channel between management and employees so the interests of both are served.

Public relations workers might take an informal survey of workers to see how they feel about their work and to find out whether they are satisfied with company policies regarding retirement benefits, vacations and promotions. If the surveys are well prepared and professionally administered, much good can come from them. Often management will learn that the majority of salespeople are dissatisfied with the commission structure, pointing up the need for a restructuring of outdated commission arrangements. By suggesting the change, the public relations staff will have set the wheels in motion to improve relations between employees and management. This encourages a better on-the-job performance by the workers.

Externally, the public relations staff has an even bigger job. Needless to say, the department store is not the only retail outlet in the city. There are least five other comparably large department stores along with hundreds of smaller retail establishments throughout the city. And they're all competing in a number of sales areas. There are small discount clothing stores downtown, for example, that slash prices regularly in order to attract customers who normally frequent department stores. There are also large warehouse-type appliance stores that sell merchandise at hefty discounts all year long. No matter where you look, our large department store faces a lot of competition.

To combat the competition, the store's public relations team is hard at work devising storewide promotions, improving community relations and designing strategies to improve the store's image.

How is it going to accomplish all that? Because the competition is so fierce, the store's management and public relations staff agree that it's important to do far more than sell merchandise in order to succeed. One solution is a number of strong promotional campaigns that will improve the store's image. One such campaign is a store-sponsored band concert on the Fourth of July. What better way to lure potential customers to the store than a free concert at the entrance to the store? Anyone is free to stop, listen and watch, and leave at any point. No one is obligated to buy a thing. The festive event creates a favorable store image that is not to be forgotten so quickly.

As for community relations, the store's management decided to contribute a large amount of money to start a day-care center in a poor section of the city. This well-thought-out strategy ultimately works to the advantage of the store and the community. When customers hear of the contribution, they will view the store as more than just another retail establishment. Now it is a store with a social conscience, one that has an obligation to the community.

So you see, each of the public relations campaigns strengthens the store's position within the city. Each one ultimately helps to boost sales.

The Public Relations of Banks

Imagine working in a business where the product offered is basically the same and the cost of the product varies little, if at all. The banking industry is unusual in this way because the product, money, is dealt with in pretty much the same manner by most banks. And what's more, banking has long been a conservative industry that prides itself on communicating a low-key image. Ask ten people to describe five major banking institutions in their city and chances are they'll describe each one in much the same way.

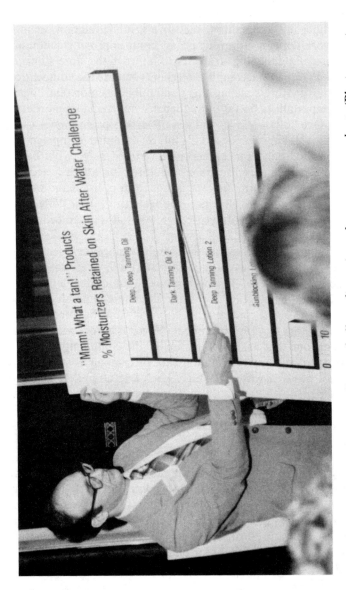

Press conference for top beauty editors of all media to introduce a new product. (Photo courtesy of Minnesota Mining and Manufacturing)

It's not hard to see why banks go out of their way to create a new image that separates one bank from another. To accomplish that end, they are spending more on public relations than they ever did in the past.

The public relations staff of a large metropolitan bank faces certain limitations that are unique to this industry. Whatever strategies are undertaken must conform to banking's conservative image. Because the product is money, something everyone cherishes and works so hard to earn, customers prefer a sedate and conservative image for the sturdy institutions that protect their money.

One important job public relations workers have undertaken is to soften banking's image and change the facade of these once-cold institutions. Next time you visit your neighborhood bank, take a look at the interior and the exterior of the building. Quite possibly the bank is located on a cheerful business street that is convenient to most people in the area. Inside you'll find modern furnishings, carpeted floors, comfortable furniture and an inviting decor. The bank's officers, tellers and even the security guards are going to go out of their way to be as friendly as possible. This all boils down to effective public relations.

A public relations campaign designed for a bank or a chain of banks, for example, might have a number of primary goals. Other than changing and lightening the image, it tries to personalize banking services and even involve the bank in community affairs. PR campaigns have ranged from special holiday programs, refreshments and entertainment served at bank openings to gifts for new depositors and fund-raising drives for worthwhile community projects.

Transportation Companies Face Special Problems

Think about the different forms of public transportation that are available to you, and the conditions under which they operate, and you can come up with some public relations strategies of your own.

What do we mean by public transportation? You guessed it —

airlines, railroads, buses and subways. The competition for passengers among the different carriers gets pretty fierce at times. Airlines, for one, are not only competing with one another but with railroads and buses as well. And buses and subways are doing their best to attract commuters going to and from work. Each one is trying to lure business its way.

Especially around holidays, airlines engage in bitter price wars with each other. The public relations staff of a domestic airline that features a number of daily flights to Florida might design a promotional package giving families a considerable discount if they take their kids along. This attracts families who might not normally take their children with them and, most important, it draws business away from competing airlines.

A PR worker employed by a railroad that crisscrosses the country has his work cut out for him in an age that has seen airlines supersede the railroads. Since time is precious, especially when you're on vacation, most travelers are reluctant to spend hours sitting on a train when they can get to their destination quickly. So it's not hard to understand why railroads are losing a great deal of money and why so many are being forced into bankruptcy. To fight the competition, major railroads are spending large sums of money on public relations in order to recover business lost to the airlines. Luxury tours tied to sizable hotel discounts might be one strategy; another is the convenience of allowing travelers to transport their automobiles along with them so they can have a means of transportation when they arrive at their destination.

Public relations for intracity bus and subway lines fall into still another category. The Metropolitan Transit Authority (MTA), the government agency that runs New York City's massive bus and subway network, is a good illustration of a sprawling intracity transportation system.

The MTA's PR staff has little time to create impressive promotional campaigns. Instead, most of their energy is spent in acting as an intermediary between commuters and MTA management. After a major subway breakdown, for instance, a press conference is hastily arranged at which MTA management is called on the carpet to explain what went wrong and what is going to be done to prevent similar accidents in the future.

It's not hard to figure out who writes the diplomatically prepared press releases as well as the speeches for MTA executives. You guessed it: the overworked public relations staff. Within hours after an accident, statements have to be made to the media and especially to angry commuters. Explanations are demanded and the public relations department has to deliver them. If the accident occurred during the evening rush hour, the PR staff resigns itself to burning the midnight oil until the job is done.

Large Industries Versus Small Industries

Rarely do you find a company that starts out big. Just as babies progress through childhood to adolescence and, eventually, reach adulthood, businesses grow in much the same way. The goal of every small business is to be a major force in its field. And naturally the public relations strategy of an emerging company is structured around building the company, improving its profits and market share and making it a significant power within its industry. Since small companies operate in a business environment dominated by giants, PR workers strive for greater visibility for their companies.

A small company is a marvelous place to get some experience if you're just starting out in the field. Instead of being thrust into a company employing thousands of employees, you're working in a more intimate setting employing a few hundred people or less. The PR department is small and is involved in all facets of the company. Within an intimate corporate setting, you either sink or swim and become a jack-of-all-trades, mastering all of them.

With a few years of experience under your belt, you have the choice of either remaining a big fish in a small but growing pool or going on to become a junior member of a PR staff of a large corporation. In either position, you have an opportunity to carve an exciting and potentially lucrative career for yourself.

Some people prefer working within a large company consisting of many tiers of command, whereas others thrive in a small company where they know each worker on a first-name basis.

Conglomerates and Multinationals

We've mentioned the differences between working for a large as opposed to a small corporation. But there are all degrees of large companies. There are multidivisional national companies that produce one product and distribute it all over the world. And there are even larger companies called conglomerates, or multinationals, which are involved in many business ventures, many of which have no relationship to one another except for the financial ties to the parent company.

Let's take a look at a large conglomerate, such as Warner Communications. To name only a few of its operations, Warner Communications is a major magazine distributor, book and magazine publisher and owner of a few successful record companies and movie studios. Its companies have divisions all over the world.

Other large conglomerates are simply referred to by their initials, such as LTV, TRW and ITT.

Since their businesses are large and complex, their public relations are a lot more sophisticated and specialized than those of smaller companies. Since they do business in many countries as well as in the United States, the public relations staffs have unique problems and objectives to contend with. For instance, establishing communication channels between management and employees throughout the world is a full-time job in itself. What with language barriers to be hurdled, distributing corporate information involves a multistep process. An important press release, for example, might have to be translated into five different languages before it can be distributed to its international divisions.

Given the gargantuan scale of the company's business, gaining public and investor recognition must also be a formidable undertaking. The sheer size of the company is an index of its public relations activities. To get the work done, the PR department is divided into different divisions to adequately cover the company's business spheres. You might find yourself working in either the publications, international, domestic or technical section of the public relations department. Or you might be involved in either the writing, account executive or speechwriting end of the business. So it stands to reason that specialization is necessary and essential in order to conduct an effective public relations campaign.

Associations

Most business people belong to 1 of 14,000 national associations. Every industry and business you can think of is represented by an association, and most of the associations are headquartered in New York City, Washington, D.C. or Chicago. Many of the large associations maintain regional offices to keep their members abreast of important developments.

Trade associations produce neither a product nor a service. Their function is to create a favorable climate for the industry they represent. There are also associations that have been established to promote or publicize a cause, such as those banning the use of nuclear power, prohibiting the killing of seals or whales, or for the purpose of dispensing information about solar energy.

In the process of promoting favorable public relations, associations have both an internal and an external function.

Internally, they keep their members abreast of activities, meetings and current developments. A large association, for example, schedules regular meetings throughout the year, and during that period members might receive a quarterly newsletter or a four- to eight-page newspaper covering industry news, promotions or legislation that affects the members.

Externally, an association works to create a favorable image for its industry as a whole and for the companies that are part of it. The steel industry, for one, maintains the Washington-based American Iron and Steel Institute, whose job is to keep the media and general public informed about developments within this broad-based industry. It publishes a variety of pamphlets and annual publications explaining how steel is made, the evolution of the industry and exciting new developments looming on the horizon.

Let's say a reporter is assigned to write a round-up story on major breakthroughs in medicine over the past few decades. There are many ways to attack this story, but a logical first step is a quick call to the American Medical Association (AMA), the prestigious organization to which most American doctors belong. The AMA's full-time staff will be more than happy to steer the reporter in the right direction, providing leads and the names of doctors and researchers who'll be delighted to furnish the information needed.

Once a reporter understands how an industry or profession works and has a feeling for who the major companies are, or where the important practitioners of a particular profession can be found, he can put together a well-researched, informative story.

Associations hire junior PR staff members. However, most trade associations prefer experienced PR workers who have a number of years of experience in the field, preferably within the industry the association services. If you've worked in the PR department of a major steel company for a number of years, for example, you might be considered an ideal candidate for the American Iron and Steel Institute.

Labor Unions

Since their inception, American trade unions have suffered from poor public relations. The reasons for this can be traced all the way back to the early beginnings of trade unionism in the United States. In those rough-and-ready days, many employers were violently opposed to unions and, as a result, brawls, broken bones and sometimes loss of human life were not uncommon due to bloody confrontations between management and union members.

Those blood-spilling days are long gone, yet union PR people still find that public opinion is mixed when it comes to controversial union issues. As one union PR staffer put it, "It depends what

Labor unions depend on the services of PR professionals. (Photo courtesy of Local 32B-32J, SEIU, AFL–CIO)

the issue is. If it's one where we have public support, such as improving working conditions for mine workers, the union is the hero because we're trying to prevent serious accidents. But if subway transit workers go on strike for higher wages and transit conditions have never been too good, commuters think the union is the villain because they're inconvenienced and they have to pay higher fares."

Depending upon the issue at hand, union public relations efforts will either have public opinion on its side or be fighting an uphill battle all the way in order to garner public sentiment.

But like other types of public relations, union PR workers have both internal and external responsibilities. As you can imagine, external PR efforts present an ongoing challenge for dedicated public relations workers. During a long and heated strike, a union's public relations staff works diligently to keep the public informed about the key issues, especially if it's a strike where public sentiment is anti-union. Along with preparing an ongoing battery of press releases explaining the union's positions, speeches have to be written for union leaders in order to keep the public informed every step of the way.

During nonstrike periods, union public relations efforts are centered around other important projects for its members. For example, most of the large powerful unions maintain offices in Washington where they employ staffs who lobby for bills that will benefit their members. PR workers might work closely with union executives in planning and designing health or retirement packages for their members.

Internally, union PR representatives have it a lot easier. Since they have the support of their members, they don't have to contend with the frustrations of trying to win public acceptance. An employee joins a union because he wants to improve his job status, gain security, earn more money and have better job benefits. In other words, most union members are delighted to be part of a unified team that is working toward goals that will benefit all employees.

PR workers face few problems in maintaining open internal communication lines between union management and members. If you were involved primarily in internal public relations, you might be preparing brochures about new programs for members, helping to publish a monthly newspaper, writing speeches for union management or preparing presentations for union-sponsored events.

The AFL-CIO, for example, maintains national, state and local news bureaus, sponsors radio and television programs, offers films and educational programs to schools and civic groups and publishes a variety of newspapers and other materials. And since organized labor is a highly specialized field, public relations representatives who work for a union tend to remain within this field throughout their careers. It requires someone who is committed to the labor movement and believes in its principles. It's not likely that someone who has been doing this type of PR work for a number of years would take a job in industrial public relations, or any other branch of public relations for that matter.

Schools and Colleges

There isn't a college or university in this country that doesn't maintain a full-time public relations staff. Like any other public relations effort, the size of the staff varies with the size of the institution. Large universities, for example, maintain multidepartment public relations teams involved in wide-ranging activities from routine fundraising and preparing of promotional literature to conceiving and implementing special projects.

How important is public relations to a college or university? Ask a college administrator that question and he or she won't be able to find enough adjectives to accurately describe its importance. One college administrator we spoke with didn't mince words and said, "Public relations is a school's bread and butter. Typically, colleges that spend a lot on public relations attract more students."

Each year millions of high school students write to colleges all over the country requesting information. They want to know everything there is to know about the school: tuition, curriculum, faculty, living arrangements and background information on the school.

Colleges are prepared to respond to these requests, and by the time winter and spring roll around, they're primed and ready to mail thousands of catalogues, brochures and applications to students requesting them. The admissions office mails the material to interested applicants, but it's the college's public relations department that collects the information, writes the copy and coordinates the graphics. That enticing college booklet or catalogue you receive in the mail is a basic PR tool used by a college or university. It is a direct, honest and straightforward promotional tool that tells a potential student at a glance whether the school is right for him or her.

But that's only one function of a college public relations department. Beyond preparing a variety of promotional literature, the school's PR department is the official information agency for the institution. Its responsibilities can be carved into the following important areas: recruitments, alumni work, special events and fund raising. Let's start with recruitment.

To lure new students to their schools, colleges send recruitment officers to selected high schools all over the country. You've probably listened to planned lectures or informal talks by college recruiters. Engineering schools, particularly, spend a great deal on recruitment since there seems to be a constant demand for engineers.

Don't be confused by the title "recruitment officer." Their job is to tell students about their school, discuss requirements, field questions and keep an eye out for potential candidates. In short, their job is 100 percent public relations. In the course of traveling about the country they meet with students, parents, and school administrators and advisors. Often students will get a better feeling for what a school is all about by talking to a recruiter than by reading the school catalogue.

Schools have discovered that a variety of promotional strategies is more effective than concentrating their efforts on a sole PR strategy.

Public relations efforts are aimed at graduates or alumni of the school as well as new students. Alumni are an excellent advertisement for the school and also a potential avenue for funds. Since it costs an enormous amount of money to run a college, a variety of fundraising efforts is essential. Most schools have alumni associations that collect membership fees as well as donations from its members. The difficult part is keeping in touch with each graduating class. It means keeping track of lists of hundreds of students and upgrading them regularly. You can see why college PR representatives working with alumni have their hands full.

Volunteer Agencies

Often referred to as nonprofit public relations, a host of agencies and organizations fall into this category. The Red Cross, Girl Scouts, Young Men's Christian Association, Cancer Society, League for the Hard of Hearing, Muscular Dystrophy, to name just a few, depend upon public contributions and grants for survival. Effective and continuous public relations are essential for these organizations if they hope to stay in business.

Nonprofit public relations concentrates most of its efforts around fundraising and enlisting public support for its cause. But like any other PR speciality, fundraising is a precise skill that requires years of training. In fact, experienced fundraisers can just about name their price. Special-purpose volunteer organizations are prepared to pay experienced fundraisers high salaries because their successful fundraising strategies often produce millions of dollars. Statistics dramatically prove this. Americans contribute about a billion dollars a year to various worthy fundraising drives.

Merely asking for money is not the way fundraisers work. That kind of approach produces disappointing results. The challenge for the public relations staffs employed by these organizations is presenting the key issues to the public in the most appropriate and tasteful manner possible. Once the key issues are presented, whether it be by way of radio, television, or newspapers and magazines, a logical fundraising drive is organized to raise money.

For example, nonprofit organizations frequently rely on special events to amass large sums of money. One highly successful special yearly event is the Muscular Dystrophy Telethon hosted by comedian Jerry Lewis. Lewis has been donating his time to this worthy cause since 1966 and has raised over $245 million for muscular dystrophy. His telethons are an annual event and people willingly give as much as they can afford to this worthy cause.

Getting a big-name personality to back a nonprofit cause is an undeniably appealing public relations strategy. Many stars willingly give a certain amount of time to their favorite causes.

The March of Dimes stages yearly bike-a-thons and walk-a-thons to raise money. Young people, especially, are asked to enlist the support of neighbors, friends and relatives to sponsor them on their walk or biking effort.

Let's say it's an 18-mile bike-a-thon, for example, and you sponsor a biker for $2 for every mile covered. If the entire course is completed, your pledge will be $36. It's quite possible for one person to raise well over $100 from a single event. Multiply that by thousands and you have what amounts to a highly successful fundraising event.

There are also all manner of professional golf and tennis tournaments staged around the country to raise money for such charities as hospitals or medical research. These attract professional sports stars as well as show-business people and they account for millions every year. All of them require the services of PR people to meet their goals.

These are only a few public relations strategies that have been successful in raising money for nonprofit organizations. There are many others. Other than planning and executing a wide variety of special events, public relations workers spend the rest of their time keeping the public informed via brochures, articles and an ongoing barrage of press releases to the media.

Public relations workers in the nonprofit sector find that they have to work hard all year long to keep their cause before the public, and more important, to keep the public enthused, interested and supportive.

Government Public Relations

Working for our government in a public relations capacity is practically the same as working for any other organization. The government also needs writers, speech writers, planners and a variety of PR specialists. The noticeable differences are in terminology and promotional techniques used.

First, our government doesn't use the word public relations. If you're employed by one of the many governmental agencies, you'd be a public information officer, official representative or spokesperson.

Since our government is a large and often unwieldy bureaucracy, public information policies and strategies are formulated slowly and it often takes months for a big public relations program to be approved. In any government agency you'll find many tiers of command. Obtaining approval for a major program can be a frustrating, not to mention time-consuming, process.

Governmental heads are very sensitive about their public information campaigns. Whether it's the Armed Forces, National Aeronautics and Space Administration (NASA), Department of Agriculture or the Food and Drug Administration, information is released to the public in a conservative and careful manner. More often than not, speeches, press releases and reports are reworded a number of times in order to satisfy the many levels of command.

To make matters more confusing, each governmental agency maintains its own public information staff and has its own way of doing things. The public information strategies employed by NASA, for instance, are quite different from those employed by the Department of the Interior or the Department of Defense. Each department has its own goals and security requirements. Public information officers employed by NASA, especially, have to be very careful about the information they release to the media. Before information is released to the press on a scheduled shuttle flight into space, for example, it's approved by a number of high-ranking officials.

Not everyone is cut out to work for a large bureaucracy like our government. You have to enjoy working for a big corporation and not mind being a small cog in a monstrous machine. In time, you can rise through the ranks, but it's also important to keep in mind that independent decision making is at a premium, since the chain of command is complicated.

Political Public Relations

A related yet very different field is political public relations. While government public relations tends to move at a snail's pace, political public relations is fast and furious, requiring snap decisions and experienced practitioners.

Simply, political public relations can be defined as the process of getting a political candidate elected, or gaining approval or support for a special issue, amendment or law.

Depending upon the size of a political campaign and the office involved, candidates invest vast sums of money in public relations. If it accomplishes its goal and captures a political office, it's money well spent. An assemblyman might spend $50,000 on a political campaign, whereas a senator running for office might spend as much as a couple of million dollars on his political campaign.

Political public relations requires a unique blend of talents. Beyond being a highly competent public relations worker, you have to be well-versed in politics. You have to understand how the political process works and the special problems involved in getting someone elected to public office. Since a background in politics is so important, many candidates seek out newspaper reporters who specialized in political reporting, either on a local or national level. Political reporters understand politics and they have a proven track record to back it up. And equally important, they have the contacts in the field.

The political public relations worker is in a class by himself because, beyond being a crackerjack writer who understands the ins and outs of politics, he or she also must be a "take charge" person who can make decisions instantly. A logical mind that can think clearly and anticipate events before they happen will be rigorously exercised by the demands of political maneuvering.

The top person running a political campaign for a senator who hopes to recapture his seat, or a president who hopes to be elected for a second term, has to have his eyes and ears open 24 hours a day. Since you're fighting to gain public support, you have to keep an eye on your opponents at all times, and you have to be prepared to change strategies and policies overnight if they are not accomplishing their goals.

During a heated political campaign, an office seeker's campaign manager is with him day and night. The hours are long and the tension can be hard to cope with. But the talented practitioners in the field love every minute of it. They relish the challenge and don't mind putting in long hours. After all, there's nothing more rewarding than designing, executing and ultimately winning a political campaign.

Not everyone in political public relations starts out as a political reporter. Many young people get some experience by doing volunteer work for a candidate. All it takes is a few political campaigns to get an idea how things work and how strategies are formulated. But it takes many more years before you're able to function on your own.

By working as a volunteer for a couple of years you can work your way into political public relations. It could take as long as ten years before you're competent enough and have sufficient contacts to actually help coordinate and run a political campaign. But the long-term rewards are well worth the hard work. Top campaign managers are well paid for their talents.

Public Relations Firms

You'll find public relations agencies (or firms) in most cities, but most of the large ones are located in large metropolitan centers such as New York and Chicago. Within these two cities alone you'll find close to 4,000 public relations firms.

Public relations firms range in size from one-person operations handling a few accounts to large firms employing several hundred people handling many different types of accounts. Essentially, there are two broad categories of public relations firms: those that specialize in a particular type of account and the general agency that handles all kinds of accounts. A specialized agency, for example, might gear itself to only financial, industrial, government or educational accounts; the generalized agency could handle accounts in all these areas.

General PR agencies are constantly changing and shifting their staffs to accommodate and service their accounts. It's quite common for an agency to drop a couple of its staff members when it loses an account, or to add a couple of people to its staff when it acquires a new account. If a general agency, for example, takes on a major chemical company and has no one on staff to administer the account, the agency will hire someone with impressive chemical credentials to handle it. In fact, many people with expertise, for example, in engineering, teaching, chemistry or mathematics, change career directions and take jobs in public relations agencies working with accounts that capitalize on their knowledge. Once they learn how a PR agency works and some of the fundamentals of the job, they find the change compatible.

But for the inexperienced person just out of school who wants to break into the field, a large public relations agency is an excellent place to start. Since large PR firms are departmentalized and employ people with different skill levels, you have the opportunity of starting at the bottom and working your way up the corporate ladder.

A large general public relations agency is carved up into a number of departments, consisting of administrative, editorial, publicity, research and production.

At the very top you have the executive, or administrative, corps who run the agency, formulate policy, and hire and fire employees. The editorial department prepares releases and stories, gathers material, interviews clients, writes picture captions and oversees the production of booklets and leaflets.

The publicity department confines itself to making arrangements such as setting up and planning interviews, contacting the media and scheduling events. If an agency's client is about to go on a speaking tour covering major universities throughout the country, the publicity department makes all the necessary arrangements.

The research department gathers material, compiles statistics and researches subjects for other staff members. If the editorial department is preparing a large booklet on the chemical industry, for instance, members of the research department gather the material from various sources so the editorial department can put the booklet together. Typically, research and editorial departments work together closely. One feeds information to the other so the work can be processed quickly and accurately.

The production department, which consists of an art director and assistants, prepares all the printed and visual material. This can mean anything from creating an entire newspaper or magazine to designing layouts for special projects such as posters, leaflets or bulletin boards.

As you can see, all the departments work closely with each other and each depends upon the others.

There are many advantages to working for a large PR agency. An inexperienced worker has the opportunity to learn how an agency works by working for different departments. With no experience, you can start out in the research department, and eventually branch out into editorial and publicity work. Or you can start out as a junior writer in the editorial department and work your way into the publicity section. Your particular skill level will determine your career direction.

In time, you can work your way up to the position of account executive (AE). The AE is an experienced PR representative who is responsible for supervising an account, or several accounts. He or she is the liaison between client and agency. If the client has a problem, wants a release rewritten or his company's PR strategy altered, the client negotiates with the AE. The AE functions very much like a high-powered salesperson, whose role is part diplomatic and part sales-oriented.

Clearly, public relations has many applications. You can work for many different types of companies and perform wide-ranging functions. When you think about all the different public relations applications, it's not hard to understand why the business depends upon people with different backgrounds, aptitudes, skill levels and talents. If you have what it takes, you can start as a "gofer" and work your way right to the very top.

4

Do You Have What It Takes?

Whether you work for an agency, corporation or nonprofit institution, public relations work is anything but dull. There is always plenty of work to keep you busy from nine to five, and it's not uncommon to put in many hours of overtime as well.

Unlike most jobs, PR work rarely adheres to a structured day. Each day is different, offering surprises and new problems to be resolved. In the next chapter we'll be zooming in on a few PR workers who work for different types of organizations. They're all involved in PR work, yet their jobs are different. Each job presents its unique pressures and obstacles. Now, let's harness our imaginations once again.

If you work for a PR agency specializing in industrial accounts, for example, you can expect to be doing many different things within the course of a week. Let's say you are the account executive for two major accounts, a cosmetics company and a food company. One part of your day will be spent working closely with your contacts at the food company and the rest of the time you'll be involved in designing promotional campaigns for the cosmetics firm. Each function is nearly a full-time job in itself. And until your company hires another account executive to take one of the accounts off your hands, you have little choice but to wear two hats.

Most of the time the pace is hectic. As one account executive employed by a large Chicago PR agency put it: "PR work is exciting and hectic enough when everything goes according to plans. However, schedules are not always met and plans don't always proceed as outlined. Inevitably, emergencies crop up when important decisions have to be made immediately."

Most seasoned PR workers are primed for the unexpected. Imagine the chaos and confusion of having to resolve pressing problems from two clients at the same time. It sounds like a nightmare, but it's a common enough occurrence in the workday of a busy PR representative.

Picture this: All of a sudden the president of the cosmetics company comes down with the flu and has to cancel a planned ten-city promotional tour. If that's not bad enough, an hour later you receive a frantic call from the product manager of the food company telling you that the promotional campaign that was about to get under way on two new products will have to be postponed because of production problems.

What do you do? The one thing you don't do is panic. No matter what happens, a PR representative must remain calm, in control and objective. As you can imagine, this is not always easy, especially if you have to deal with problems such as those outlined above.

The first thing that runs through your mind is whether you'll be able to resolve all the problems. But having been in similar situations before, you've learned that panicking is fruitless and the only effective way to resolve situations like this to keep a clear head and try to come up with workable solutions.

Fifteen minutes of careful reflection is all you need to think of temporary solutions. Instead of cancelling the planned promotional tour for the head of the cosmetics company, you suggest that the executive vice-president, along with a key member of your PR staff, go instead. That way everything can proceed on schedule. And to give your food company more time to straighten out its production problems, you discover that you're able to halt the promotional machinery just before press releases and product kits are mailed out to the media. Quick, calm, deliberate thinking helps you to ward off two potential crisis situations. Things looked mighty bleak for a few unnerving moments until you were able to find ways out of the dilemmas.

Personal Qualifications

Not everyone can work in tense situations like the one just described. Some of us prefer stable work situations where job routines vary little from day to day. The preceding situations are not uncommon in public relations work. Remember: As a public relations person, your first obligation is to your client. If a crisis arises your responsibility is to solve it. And more often than not, accommodating your client means putting in bizarre hours.

Another dramatic situation comes to mind where public relations workers had to act fast. A few years ago a plane carrying over 80 passengers exploded while taking off and almost all of the passengers died in the crash. Within minutes of the accident the news swept around the world. The same questions bolted through everyone's mind. What happened? Why did a major airline with a faultless track record lose a plane? Whose fault was it? Was it human or mechanical error? Explanations were demanded. The airline's executive board and public relations people were summoned to prepare statements to be released to the media. It was a tense situation. The problem was that no one, not even officials from the airline that lost the plane, could begin to evaluate the situation at that point. Yet answers were demanded and a statement had to be prepared at once. You can just imagine what the tension was like when management and public relations staff members met to decide on a course of action. Telephones rang continuously, while the PR staff, working closely with airline engineers and technical experts, prepared a series of statements that attempted to explain what had happened. They worked around the clock until they were ready to release enough information about the crash.

Thankfully, plane crashes don't happen too often. But when

they do, explanations have to be made immediately. Since the public relations staff is the airline's information arm, they are the ones who have to answer to the media and public.

Self-Evaluation Test

As you can see, public relations is not for everyone. It requires special talents, abilities and emotional stability. To find out whether you have the necessary attributes to work in public relations, answer "yes" or "no" to the following questions and see how well you do.

Public Relations Profile

1. Can you work well under pressure? _____
2. Do you enjoy challenging situations? _____
3. Can you take criticism? _____
4. Are you an organized person? _____
5. Do you work well with people? _____
6. Do you consider yourself an articulate person? _____
7. Do you have a good imagination? _____
8. Are you sensitive to other people's feelings? _____
9. Can you make snap decisions and carry them through? _____
10. Do you have good judgment? _____
11. Do you have leadership capabilities? _____
12. Are you a good salesperson? _____
13. Does it upset you to work unconventional hours? _____
14. Do you enjoy doing several things at once? _____

Let's take a look at each question and see how it relates to public relations work.

Can you work under pressure?

If your answer was no, you should strongly question whether

public relations is the field for you. No one enjoys working under pressure all the time, yet it is something PR workers have to contend with. It's safe to say that all public relations workers, regardless of the field, have to deal with a certain amount of on-the-job pressure. Some fields, such as entertainment or certain government and corporate PR that are involved with national security or high-priority products, are more apt to be high-pressure fields than others. As mentioned earlier, PR workers employed by transportation companies have more pressures to contend with than other public relations workers.

Some of us can tolerate a great deal of pressure; others cannot. Many workers find a certain amount of pressure stimulating; others recoil in the face of it. Pressure can be crippling if you don't know how to cope with it. Some fields have more than their fair share of on-the-job pressures. Advertising, public relations and journalism (print and broadcast), for example, are high-pressure fields.

Pressure is an inescapable part of PR work, and it's a good idea to come to terms with that element of the job before you seriously pursue the field.

Do you enjoy challenging situations?

Challenge is a PR worker's middle name. No matter what aspect of public relations work you're involved in, you can expect challenge every step of the way. That applies to the agency's role in trying to acquire new clients, the account executive's part in acting as the creative middleperson between agency and client, and the PR writer/strategist who designs promotional campaigns, prepares press kits and distributes promotional literature.

In highly competitive areas, such as entertainment and industrial PR, the overriding challenge is often to merely hold on to the account. PR agencies are performing a service which the client pays for. If the agency fails to meet its obligations and does not service the account properly, the client dismisses the agency. If it's an account that produces enormously high revenues for the agency (such

Working on a magazine layout for a PR firm involves painstaking care and attention to detail. (Photo courtesy of Vista)

as a major oil company the likes of Mobil or an international conglomerate like Warner Communications), heads will roll and a number of PR representatives will find themselves out on the street looking for new jobs. So PR work is anything but dull.

Can you take criticism?

In the process of working your way up the career ladder, you have to be prepared to accept and profit from criticism. As we said earlier when discussing the process of preparing a tight, tersely written press release, junior writers can spend hours preparing a single press release. When that release is completed, it's often heavily edited, and sometimes rewritten by a senior member of the staff. That's how junior writers become senior writers, and senior writers go on to become administrators.

Not everyone absorbs criticism the same way. Some of us are not able to separate our egos from our work and take criticism personally. Others, however, are able to absorb it and learn from it. If you view criticism as part of the process of mastering your job, you'll be able to move ahead quickly.

Being able to absorb criticism is an important part of public relations work. In fact, you can expect it on all levels, not just as a junior writer or researcher. Account executives have to field criticism from their clients. The first person a client complains to is not the head of the PR agency, but the AE servicing the account.

As in advertising, criticism in public relations often operates in a boomerang syndrome. If a client is not satisfied with the way a promotional campaign is going, he'll call up his AE and complain. Naturally, the AE is upset and apologetic and promises to straighten out the situation immediately. "It's as good as taken care of," he says to the client cordially, promising to be back to him within the hour with some changes and recommendations. Our AE appears calm and confident. But that's only the external appearance. Underneath, he's seething because he feels other staff members didn't prepare the client's PR campaign to specifications. Seconds after he hangs up the phone he barges into the editor in chief's office to find out why the campaign didn't meet client expectations. The editor in chief is now upset and calls in the writer who prepared the press release and promotional literature. And on and on down the ladder.

As you can see, criticism has a way of rebounding until everyone is involved. Yet, there are good reasons for it. If the problems are not solved, the agency stands to lose the account.

Are you an organized person?

In a busy public relations firm you can expect to be doing a number of things at once. Planning, coordination and organization are essential. No matter what department you work for you'll have deadlines to contend with.

If you're a PR writer working on three accounts at the same time, you might be facing a series of deadlines. Two press releases might be due in three days, while the following week a press kit and lengthy interview are scheduled to be presented to your clients for approval. Your days are hectic and crammed with work. To get it all done, organization is essential.

An account executive also faces organizational problems. If a number of your clients are clamoring for their promotional literature and demand attention immediately, as AE you have to find that harmonious chord which will satisfy all of them.

PR work requires an organized person who can create workable and flexible systems that permit him to get the work done. Without system and organization, you'll be wallowing in confusion and will never get anything done on time.

Do you work well with people?

Public relations is a people business. Whether you work in non-profit, corporate, government or agency PR, you'll be interacting with people most of the day. In an agency, for example, you'll work closely with fellow staff members and clients. Each relationship is different and requires a different kind of input. When working with staff members, your goal is to get the work done on time and to client specifications.

In a large public relations agency account executives, art directors, publicity, editorial and administrative personnel all work together. In sum, within any business day, you'll be talking and dealing with dozens of different people.

The client relationship is a little different. Here, flexibility, understanding and sensitivity to the business relationship are essential. Your job is to maintain a friendly and productive relationship at all times. This isn't always easy. Not every client is going to be that easy to deal with. While the majority of your clients will present few problems, others may be demanding and difficult to work with. The challenge is being able to deal with all of them. Again, the experienced PR worker can work productively with all clients, regardless of their personalities or their outrageous demands.

As the head of one small PR agency that specializes in industrial accounts said, "Working with people is an art. It's a lot harder than a lot of people realize."

What it all means is that PR representatives have to use tact and diplomacy as skillfully as they use words in maintaining productive business relationships.

Do you consider yourself an articulate person?

PR people communicate on many different levels. In the course of a business day, you might be writing, speaking and coordinating various projects. Part of your day might be confined to writing, while the remainder of the day you're in conferences or working directly with clients.

Account executives, for example, spend the better part of their day working with clients. Since they are the liaison between agency and client, they need good verbal skills and an easygoing, persuasive manner.

Being with and talking to people comes easily to PR people. They are good at it and enjoy doing it. Like salespeople in other businesses, they enjoy communicating on a one-to-one basis. Some of us are better at this than others. You've heard the expression, "He's a born salesman." That statement can be true. For some, verbal communication comes naturally, while others have to work a little harder at it before they can get to the stage where they interact comfortably with others.

A confident AE, for instance, feels comfortable with anyone and is able to communicate effortlessly. In fact, junior PR workers are often amazed at how easily experienced AEs get along with people. They are very much like experienced actors and actresses who can portray a variety of characters at a moment's notice. This trait is a real asset when working for a general PR agency with many different types of accounts. In the course of a workweek, you might be dealing with nuclear physicists, car salespeople, chemists and construction engineers. Each group is different, yet the experienced PR person is able to get along with all of them. It's not easy and for some it takes years to develop this ability.

Do you have a good imagination?

Hopefully, your answer was yes. By now you know PR workers wear many different hats. In every sense of the word they are Renaissance people who pride themselves on being multifaceted. You have to be prepared to use your imagination in order to formulate a strategy that best meets your client's objectives.

Every product and service requires a unique PR strategy. The challenging part is devising a suitable PR campaign for your client's product. Would you promote perfume, breakfast cereal and designer jeans the same way? The answer is a resounding *no*.

If it's a big account, such as Dow Chemical, General Foods, U.S. Steel or International Business Machines (IBM), it's quite common for several PR agencies to bid for the account. This is where creativity comes into play. If a number of major PR agencies are bidding for these prestigious accounts, they will do everything in their power to impress these potential clients with creative and innovative public relations strategies.

Do You Have What It Takes?

Are you sensitive to other people's feelings?

Hopefully, another yes. When working closely with people, it's essential that you be sensitive to and respect their feelings. Again, PR people carry on many different types of relationships. They have to work closely with their own staffs, and on the other hand they have to maintain a productive and professional relationship with their clients. Yet, in each encounter, sensitivity and understanding are called for. When working with a client, for instance, you have to practically anticipate problems and questions before they occur. A good AE tries his best to be one step ahead of his client. A fruitful and lasting relationship is one in which the PR person structures and directs the relationship. During a tense, nerve-racking campaign, an AE, for example, might have to do some creative hand-holding in order to get his client through a tough period. It stands to reason that a client would be nervous if he has invested close to a million dollars in a publicity campaign. As the AE on the account, part of your job is to reassure your client and help him through trying periods. After all, if an elaborate PR campaign fails dismally, millions of dollars could be lost. So it's important that PR worker and client maintain an open, understanding and professional relationship at all times.

Can you make snap decisions and carry them through until completed?

In the words of one high-ranking PR writer, "A public relations worker has to be a 'take charge' person." No truer words were ever spoken. "Take charge" means being able to get things done quickly and efficiently. It also means being able to look at a situation, analyze it and be able to make a decision. Experienced PR workers do this all the time.

Often, in the course of a political campaign, for example, decisions have to be made instantly by the campaign manager. If your client is trying to snare a senate seat and his opponent is gaining ground, you might have to resort to a new and more drastic

71

strategy. This might mean changing course midstream and restructuring your client's campaign strategy.

Time is often a luxury PR workers don't have. If you work for a big New York PR agency, for example, and your agency is bidding for a major oil account, chances are you have to work fast and furiously to get the account. If you're the one who is expected to come up with the strategy that will win the account over, you probably won't have too much time to work on the campaign. The pressure is on *you* to formulate a PR campaign that will capture this million-dollar account. Here again, quick, resourceful and creative thinking is called for.

Do you have good judgment?

Along with the ability to make snap decisions, good judgment is called for as well. In a client-agency relationship, you, the AE, are the expert when it comes to formulating strategy and analyzing the market. You are the one who has to guide the client along and help him make decisions. Good judgment and an understanding of the marketplace are crucial.

If your account is a new toy company that plans on introducing a new mechanical robot on the market, part of your job is to analyze the toy robot market and make prudent market decisions regarding the most effective sales strategy to employ to introduce the product to the public.

Do you have leadership capabilities?

Few of us are born leaders. For most of us, it's an acquired trait. Yet, leadership abilities are an asset in any job, especially public relations. Agency heads and account executives have to have leadership abilities. Once an important decision is made, they have to make sure that decision is carried out to client specifications. It often means coordinating massive campaigns employing hundreds of people, and directing them and guiding them until the project is completed.

Junior PR workers develop this trait through working and dealing with people on a day-to-day basis. It's not something that is learned overnight. With experience and confidence comes the ability to administer and lead a campaign so that it fulfills a client's goals.

Are you a good salesperson?

PR workers have to have salesmanship skills. Instead of selling a product, you are selling your services.

Before you even land a job with a PR agency or corporation, you have to convince your potential employer that you are the person for the job. You have to radiate confidence and self-assurance. You have to be able to sell yourself. And once you get the job, your next selling effort is capturing new accounts and maintaining existing ones. They all involve salesmanship abilities in one way or another. If you are bidding for a new account, you have to make a convincing case to a prospective client that your particular PR approach is the one that is going to successfully introduce and sell the product. Here again, a variety of PR skills come into play — salesmanship, confidence, good judgment, verbal skills and knowledge of your product.

A successful PR representative has to be a high-powered salesperson. First he has to believe in the product or service he is selling, and second, he has to convince others that it is the very best on the market.

Does it upset you to work unconventional hours?

There is nothing conventional about public relations work, least of all the hours.

What is different about PR work are the unknowns. It's hard to say beforehand how a workweek will proceed. Often you'll be working a normal nine-to-five day. However, there will be countless days when you'll be coming in at eight and leaving at seven and sometimes you'll have to put in a few hours on Saturday as well.

A client may come into town unexpectedly, and it might mean a dinner meeting or a Saturday breakfast meeting. Or a client may be dissatisfied with a promotional campaign and you'll have to do some emergency revision work. This boils down to an unexpected three to four hours of overtime work.

Or, if you're frantically trying to get your corporate newspaper in the mail on time, you might have to put in a few hours of work to get it done.

No matter how you look at it, there is no such thing as a typical work day in public relations.

Do you enjoy doing several things at once?

A busy PR person is inevitably involved in several projects at the same time. If you're at the writing end of the business, you can expect to be coordinating several projects at once. You might be writing three press releases at different points during the day while gathering information for stories that are scheduled to appear in the company house organ. If you're an AE, you might be supervising three separate accounts while outlining strategies for two potential accounts. And if you're the head of the agency, no doubt you'll have your hands in every department and know what every staff member is doing.

PR workers enjoy being busy. All things considered, the unconventional work routines offer excitement and challenge found in very few businesses. Although the pace can get frantic at times, PR people couldn't imagine doing anything else with their time.

5

The PR Worker's Typical Day

Brian Perry is representative of the younger generation in the public relations field. He's in his late 20s and, after studying journalism in college, worked for several weekly newspapers on the Eastern Seaboard.

After that he switched to writing and editing a national Sunday newspaper supplement for two years. He is something of a jack-of-all-trades because along the way he picked up all the skills you need to make it in PR: writing, reporting, interviewing and photography. He has held his current job for about two years and he couldn't be happier with it even though it often involves long hours and sometimes working at home.

Life in Labor PR

Brian is a busy man. He's kept hopping from the time he gets to work in the morning until he turns off his desk lamp at the end of what can often be a very long business day.

He works in public relations for a local of the Service Employees International, AFL-CIO, and as he says, "My job is anything but dull. I doubt if I could last in a job where I had to do the same thing day after day. Here I get a chance to do a million and one things.

It's more exciting this way. It keeps my adrenalin flowing all the time.''

Variety and challenge are two facets of the job he likes the best. In any given week he will help to put together the local's newspaper, write press releases and reports, prepare speeches, design leaflets, cover meetings, and monitor the media for any mention that might be of interest to the union he represents.

As a public relations worker for the AFL-CIO, Brian is involved in a somewhat specialized area of the business. There are many elements involved in his work, yet his overall function is to keep his union's members informed about issues and events that might directly affect them. Each project in which he is involved represents an information avenue of its own.

While public relations workers specialize in many different fields and are employed by every conceivable industry, the name of the game is still communication. Competent pros pride themselves on their ability to exchange information in concise, clear, understandable terms. As Brian Perry puts it:

"The AFL-CIO is a big union and, because we have members all over the country, it's not always easy staying on top of news items that affect our members. While I'm involved in local issues, I also have to work closely with the international division, which covers the whole country.

"So we have news and information on two fronts: local and international," he says.

Every month Brian helps coordinate the union's newspaper, which is distributed throughout the greater New York area. Depending on the amount of news that has to be reported, the paper can run anywhere from 8 to 28 pages.

"Most of the time our paper is pretty small," says Brian, "because we're just covering local issues. Around holiday time, it usually gets fatter because there's more news — meetings and conferences and issues that all have to be covered."

Reporting on recent developments is only a small part of the job. Once the stories are all written and the photographs processed, the paper has to be laid out, printed and distributed, and that's a time-consuming job. Almost before one issue is in the mail, Brian is working on the next one.

Press Releases

Press releases are prepared when there is a significant news event that justifies them. "We don't prepare press releases every time something happens," says Brian. "It's usually devoted to something important that affects all of our members and we want to let people know about it right away.

"For instance, if the union is announcing a program or taking a position on an issue that concerns the union's members, we'll send out a press release. I've learned that it serves little purpose to send out press releases every time we have a routine announcement.

"It has to be something significant or else news people won't take it seriously. The purpose of a release is to get immediate coverage. That's why it's crucial to send them to newspaper and magazine editors who will read them and use them."

The best that Brian can hope for from a press release is that an editor will think the item is important enough to justify writing a full story about it.

"Just having a release rewritten or printed as is, is terrific," he says. "But when an editor thinks the issue is important enough to do a full story, we're delighted because we've accomplished what we set out to do."

Maintaining Contacts

"It's great when you have some contacts at a newspaper," says Brian. "That makes it a lot easier when you have to pitch stories. Most public relations workers have a battery of contacts which they have developed over the years.

"It's a lot easier proposing ideas when you know an editor on a first-name basis. If I feel a story is right for a certain magazine, for example, I'll call my contact and discuss the idea. If the editor likes it, we'll get together or I'll send along more information and eventually — and hopefully — it leads to a published story.

"The difficult part is calling up an editor or writer cold. This takes a little practice. Editors are busy people and they don't like to waste time on the telephone. When I call up someone I don't know, I try to get to the point as quickly as possible. That way they don't feel like I'm taking up their time.

"The most effective way to deal with editors is to write them first. You outline the story for them and tell them why you think it would be useful for their readers. At the end of letters like this I usually add that I'll call them in a few days if I don't hear from them. That way I haven't put them on the spot and they can think about the proposal when they have the time.

"More often than not, I get a call within a few days after they get the letter," he says.

From time to time, Brian is called on to write speeches for the local's president. High-ranking officals, whether they work for a union, corporation or association, rarely have the time to sit down and write their own speeches.

More often a speech is the result of the combined efforts of the PR writer and the executive, with the public relations people doing all the actual writing.

"Speech writing can be tricky," Brian says. "People don't write and speak the same way. When I first tried to write a speech it sounded long-winded and preachy — more like a report than a speech.

"A well-written speech has to sound as if one person is talking informally to other people. The sentences have to be short, interesting and full of stories and anecdotes. And if you can inject a little humor, all the better. The idea is to establish rapport with your listeners and then hold their interest.

"A lot of creativity goes into writing a speech," Brian says. "To write a good one, you have to know the person you're writing for. You have to know his mannerisms and approach and you have to use the words that he would use.

"In other words, you have to pretend that you *are* the person you're writing for. I usually rewrite a speech a few times before I'm satisfied with it. Then I give it to the person I've written it for and he usually makes some changes. Then I rewrite it again."

All of this is extremely time-consuming. There are constant deadlines and a lot of frustration. It's easy to see how Brian's day flies by. On really busy days he barely has time to grab a fast lunch at a nearby luncheonette.

"Usually I munch away at a sandwich and sip a container of coffee at my desk while I'm doing a million different things. The phones never stop ringing, but I wouldn't have it any other way. Taking work home used to bother me at first, but it doesn't anymore. It's all part of this business," he says.

Nonprofit Work

Mary Blue Magruder took a rather roundabout route into public relations and it certainly wasn't typical. She is the director of development for an organization called Earthwatch in Belmont, Massachusetts.

Earthwatch is a nonprofit operation that funds scientific expeditions around the world. It recruits people who pay their own way to travel with and help scientists in their research work around the globe.

Earthwatch's travel itinerary reads like a Rand-McNally atlas, with some of its expeditions going to countries that few people have ever heard of. How did Mary Blue Magruder wind up there? By sheer coincidence, to hear her tell it.

"I was a Renaissance history major at Harvard. I have absolutely no journalism experience. I guess you could say I'm self-taught. I studied a little bit of this and little bit of that — biochemistry, history, economics — and I got a job with a management consulting firm in New York," she says.

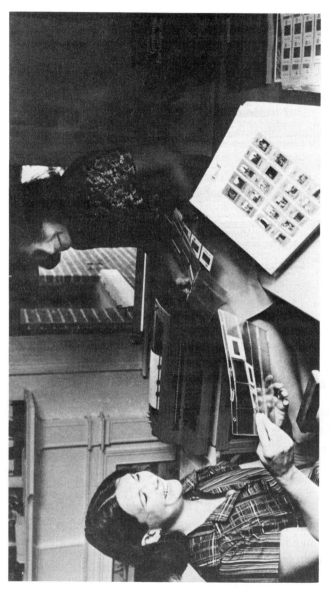

"Blue" Magruder, left, is director of development for a nonprofit organization called Earthwatch in Boston. It has sponsored over 400 projects in 55 countries. Here her assistant helps her choose slides for a magazine article. (Photo courtesy of Earthwatch)

Know your subject matter is Ms. Magruder's advice to PR job seekers. On this trip into aboriginal Australia she practices what she preaches, downing something called a witchety grub. She says it tastes like egg yolk . . . sort of. (Photo courtesy of Earthwatch)

"I did a lot of reports, press releases, public relations-related things, and I wound up at the American Health Foundation after a while."

From the Foundation she went to Earthwatch about five years ago and has since been involved in all manner of things. In 1981 alone, she was responsible for some 350 published articles about the activities of Earthwatch, which operates on a $1.5 million annual budget.

"It's a matter of dreaming up angles. A reporter will call me up when he's on a deadline and ask me if I know a vulcanologist he can call for a piece on Mt. St. Helen's. Someone else may need an expert on coastal mining," she says.

"Blue" Magruder, as she is called, handles the Earthwatch educational program and works closely with both museums and the press, including radio and television appearances for Earthwatch scientists.

"Usually, I'm behind the scenes, but I do some radio and television work. My biggest audience was three million on an Australian TV show," she says.

Her other duties include organizing lecture tours for Earthwatch scientists, public service advertising, getting the organization mentioned in the corporate press, and preparing brochures.

Although she may have been largely self-taught, Ms. Magruder learned rapidly. She has a few tips for people interested in performing well in public relations:

1. Be honest.
2. Don't exaggerate.
3. Know your market — know the audience you are trying to reach.
4. Know the pros and cons of a subject.

"I don't really like to write," she says, "but I can dream up some pretty good ideas for freelance writers to follow through on. Some people deal in words, other people deal in ideas," she says.

In case you were thinking that public relations is a high-powered travel field, think again. It's high-powered all right, but even in a job like Blue Magruder's there isn't that much travel. The best she's done in her behind-the-scenes jobs are trips to Nepal and Australia.

Corporate PR

Al DeCicco is a senior public relations specialist with the Minnesota Mining and Manufacturing Co. (3M) office in New York City. He is also what you might call a generalist. DeCicco didn't study public relations and he didn't go to journalism school either.

He worked his way up the corporate ladder in a steady progression. He began as a general assignment reporter for the Rochester, N.Y.-based Gannett newspaper chain. Later he was a copy desk editor for the *New York Times.*

Along the way he picked up an expertise in household do-it-yourself information and wrote hundreds of columns on that subject for the New York *Daily News.* He also worked for a New York advertising firm before joining 3M several years ago.

DeCicco, who's done well enough in the business to have a weekend home on the Maine coast, is not really a fan of colleges that teach public relations. He is fond of telling lecture audiences that you have to learn the ground rules before you can learn the techniques of this profession.

He thinks that much of the media's attitude toward public relations is the result of misunderstanding its role. "A lot of people have this mental picture of the hotshot PR man wheeling and dealing at fancy luncheons and dinner parties. It just isn't that way at all," he says. "It's a lot of hard work. There's no such thing as a structured workweek. You can get to the office Monday morning and write two lists of things you want to accomplish that week.

"I usually write 'imperative' over one column and 'important' over the other one. Then the phones start ringing and you can throw those lists in the wastebasket.

"I think it's important to plan your days beforehand. But you can't be rigid about it, because inevitably plans have to be altered along the way. I've learned to be flexible. That way, if things don't work out, you're not devastated. More often than not, I'm accomplishing what I intended to do after five o'clock.''

Take history or journalism or economics or political science in college, with a few courses as a minor in communications or public relations — that's DeCicco's advice.

"A good public relations person, no matter what end of the field he's in, should have good old-fashioned common sense and present a good image," he says.

"Remember, you can't just talk about the good things; you have to present the bad along with them. Consumers today are too sophisticated to fool for very long. That's true whether you're trying to sell a product or an image."

DeCicco should know. Several years ago, before he joined Minnesota Mining, he worked for an agency whose task it was to lure industries from the North to the state of South Carolina, where taxes and operating costs were far lower.

"Back in the 1970's the public image of South Carolina was that it was something right out of *Tobacco Road*. It wasn't, of course, but that's what people thought. What we had to do was to tell companies all over the country that we had the workers. We had to stress the advantages, very real advantages, of what we had to offer," he says.

And that was what he managed to do for the Industrial Development Board of the state of South Carolina through a series of newspaper and magazine articles and the judicious placement of public figures on radio and TV shows. All that was designed to alter the image of the state.

And alter it DeCicco did. South Carolina lured millions of dollars worth of business and industry away from the New York and New England area, and South Carolina, its image radically changed, couldn't be happier about it.

Tools of the Trade

The PR person's best friend is the typewriter. "Know your

typewriter," DeCicco is fond of saying. "You can study all the marketing and business education courses you want, but if you can't write, forget it."

In DeCicco's end of the business, public relations is used as a marketing tool. In essence, PR is used to solve marketing problems, he says. For instance, 3M had a line of sanding wheels which weren't moving all that well, primarily because hardware store owners used to display them in their paint departments. By moving them to the much more visible and attractive display areas that included power tools, 3M boosted its sales of the wheels. Problem solved.

An analogy of this problem-solving technique that DeCicco likes has to do with insurance: "For years, people were told that they needed insurance. They knew they needed it but they didn't really understand it and they didn't really know why. It was a good public relations campaign that explained insurance and *told* them why. Look at today's TV commercials for the big insurance companies. Their image has been changed."

When DeCicco says that you should know your typewriter, he isn't kidding. In a typical week he, or some of his co-workers, might be called upon to write a PR program for anything from Scotch tape to sandpaper. There are press kits for all manner of things, from marinas to power tools; there are outlines for television and trade magazine interviews to be set up.

DeCicco estimates that he works somewhere between 50 and 60 hours a week. He's no stranger to juggling papers and reports on a commuter train, and he's no stranger to constant travel, either. He figures that he spends some 20 percent of his time on the road, mostly flying between St. Paul, Minnesota — the corporate headquarters of 3M — and New York.

He is a man who can handle product public relations for anything from soap to tractors. He can and has written speeches and audio/visual presentations. He is a generalist in the true sense of the word. This is what he'll tell you about the public relations business. It may be the best advice you'll ever get:

"Most agencies and corporate public relations operations today won't hire you without four to five years of newspaper experience. They teach you to be a generalist. They teach you how to cope with deadline pressure. Deadlines are important. You have to learn how to handle them.

"You have to know how to organize your time. I'm not sure that this is something that you can learn in school, which is why so many good public relations people come from a newspaper background."

Airline Public Relations

Jim Ashlock is an affable Texan who is the news bureau director for Eastern Airlines at the International Airport in Miami, Florida. You want to know about his job? Listen to what he wrote in the Columbia Journalism School's newsletter in New York recently:

"A few interesting wrinkles during the year. The *Miami Herald* did a piece on me as spokesman for the area's No. 1 employer and I endured considerable exposure on the wires and TV responding to queries about the PATCO (Professional Air Traffic Controllers Organization) strike, airline fare wars and all the other stuff that seems to make news.

"I'm also teaching courses in public relations for Barry College (in Florida) and Embry-Riddle Aeronautical University, just to see whether teaching might be worthwhile for me sometime in the future."

Ashlock is fairly typical of many public relations people. He came to the job via daily newspapers and the thought of teaching the art grows more and more attractive to him.

He recognizes that this sort of instruction has more than its share of problems. He says that when he gets resumes from hopeful young people interested in a public relations career, he tells them not to be in a big hurry to strike it rich in the wonderful world of PR.

"The first thing you're looking for is a good writer and the only way I know of to learn to be one is with a news background. You can't teach people how to write, but you can teach them how to communicate and that's the name of this game. If there's one word that sums up public relations it's 'communication,'" he says.

"There's a lot of drama and romance that somehow got attached to this business. I really don't know why. But what people who want to go into it have to remember is that you have to master the essential tools," he says.

Handling public relations for one of the country's major air carriers is not easy. This is a high-risk, high-visibility profession. One learns to live with the possibility of catastrophic events like crashes or crippling strikes that affect a lot of people. As Ashlock says: "We're on call 24 hours a day. They can call you day or night, and they do."

He's generally in the office by 8 or so in the morning. He doesn't leave until 6 and he fields perhaps as many as 40 telephone calls a day. "It's a response-type job. You respond to whatever the situation happens to be and you have to do it quickly," he says.

Ashlock detests the word "image." He prefers the word "reputation." And that's what he thinks PR is all about — building a corporation's reputation.

"You have to remember that the media can get down on a company," he says. "You have to remember that and you have to avoid that."

During his busy day his functions are many. His primary responsibility is corporate. But, on top of that, there are media relations, internal communications and the general role of providing marketing support for Eastern. The way he describes it is:

"We're not into sales promotion. We play an information role. We precede and supplement the advertising department.

"Don't misunderstand me. It's a lot of fun. But when I get a letter for a job from a young person, I have to deal with the realities of a situation in which neither I nor anyone on my staff has the time to train them or to teach them."

That's why he tells young job applicants that if they go right from college to the PR department of a big corporation that they might be disappointed. Instead, he advises, go out and work at something that you really like, "something you really get a buzz out of. Learn the basics, build up a reputation, then come to a big company."

Ashlock himself is probably his own best example. He was nuts about aircraft. He'd fly anything he could climb into and thought might make it off the ground. He knew from the start that he wanted to work with something that involved planes.

He flew them and he wrote about them and, in short, he learned his trade.

That's how he wound up at Eastern.

6

What To Study — What You'll Make

Dr. Ray E. Hiebert runs a company called Communication Research Associates, Inc., in College Park, Maryland. He is also a professor of journalism who splits his time between teaching and running his research and consulting firm.

He was the advisory editor of two books, *Organizational Communications* and *Informing the People,* wrote several books in the field of mass communications and teaches in the University of Maryland's public relations program. According to Hiebert, the four-year PR curriculum is not exactly what you might expect. Much of it is literally grafted to a journalism program.

"In the first two years, the program is 75 percent liberal arts. The people we get study things like science, math, political science, sociology, psychology, economics, statistics, history, literature and journalism," he says.

In the third and fourth year at Maryland, which offers a PR curriculum that is fairly standard, courses include such features as an introduction to mass communications, writing for the mass media, news reporting and editing, and the principles of public relations.

The Maryland school uses a case-problem system to teach such concepts as the historical role of public relations and how, through the years, public opinion has been shaped by the mass media.

One of the courses, generally given in the third year, includes in-

Artistic skills are a plus. Don't let anyone tell you that you can get by with only a typewriter and your wits. (Photo courtesy of Real World Photos)

struction in public relations techniques such as how to write press releases and write for house organs or internal corporate magazines. There are lessons in how to stage events like press parties and other promotional campaigns. The students also learn about the sometimes bewildering world of press relations and the far more intricate subject of employee relations.

"At the start of their third year, the students have to choose one of four courses — photography, the laws of mass communications, broadcasting or advertising," Dr. Hiebert says.

"Basically, what we're trying to produce here are good writers and editors. A lot of people think that this is a glamor industry where everyone spends three-hour, three-martini lunches with the client. But that's not true. It's a lot of hard work that often doesn't get enough respect.

"One of the troubles with public relations is that there are too many people in it who just don't know their subject. You have to know what it is you're trying to put across before you can put it across," Dr. Hiebert says.

One way to do that is to encourage internships which involve the Maryland students in on-the-job training with radio and TV stations or with functioning public relations firms.

"We've had summer interns working not only in the Baltimore and Washington area but in New York, Philadelphia, Oklahoma and even an English-language radio station in Korea," says Dr. Hiebert.

"Public relations is still a very attractive field. It draws a lot of people who go into dozens of different areas of the field."

Dr. Hiebert says that most of the Maryland graduates go into such areas as government and politics, trade associations, corporations, counseling firms and schools, hospitals and religious organizations. The last three, he says, have recently become quite popular with people seeking entry-level jobs.

It's not easy to make it to the top, he says. Even someone with a four-year bachelor's degree from a school like Maryland will start out writing employee newsletters for a big company, churning out press releases or writing for a company magazine.

What's the competition like? It's tough. Very tough, because, as Dr. Hiebert says, "There are an awful lot of people going into public relations today. If you stick it out, you can do very well. Today, students are much more job-oriented than they used to be. They're much more concerned with where they're going to be ten years down the road."

The normal way to the top is to graduate from writing press releases to running an internal communications organ or information service, handling your own account or branching out into business for yourself.

The pay can vary widely. Dr. Hiebert notes that his graduates generally start at between $12,000 and $15,000, although some have been known to command salaries in the $18,000 to $20,000 range. Sometimes that's a matter of luck, but more often it's a matter of one's ability to master the skills of communication. Nothing comes very easily in this highly competitive field where salaries, from top to bottom, can fluctuate wildly.

Salary Ranges

It's in the salary area that public relations becomes fascinating. According to published figures from Marshall Consultants in New York City, a person holding the title of vice-president or director of public relations in corporate communications, corporate relations or public affairs will pull down somewhere between $80,000 and $150,000.

In the $50,000 to $125,000 range are such staff jobs as government relations, investor relations, press relations, editorial services, consumer affairs, international affairs, community affairs, employee relations, and issues management or division public relations director.

The picture isn't exactly bad in the public relations counseling firms where the principal officer could make from $100,000 to $200,000 and more, an executive vice-president or senior vice-president between $75,000 and $150,000, and a group vice-president or manager roughly $50,000 to $100,000.

The figures above have to do, of course, with people who have had sufficient luck, skill and experience to reach the top level of the profession.

The PR Reporter in Exeter, New Hampshire, breaks down the median salaries of top level PR practitioners according to the type of organization for which they work.

In public relations firms the median is $45,000; in advertising agencies it's $36,500; in other consulting firms, $38,000; in banks, $34,000; insurance companies, $29,500; consumer product companies, $37,500; industrial firms, $36,000; conglomerates, $42,000; transportation, $33,800; utilities, $36,500; hospitals, $23,650; educational facilities, $27,700; trade or professional associations, $36,000; and government, $29,000.

You should know that these figures can vary widely from one part of the country to another. They're highest in the Northeast, where the median salary is $38,000, and the lowest in the West, where that figure drops to $24,500.

In the North Central states the median pay is $32,000, and in the South the figure is $31,500.

A Woman's World?

More than one witty soul has called public relations the "Velvet Ghetto," an allusion to the fact that this presumably glamorous field has recently attracted more and more women. Many of them have made it to the corporate top and earn big money.

Experts cite the fact that in the last four years more than one half of the college students studying public relations have been women. Extending this figure, many such experts feel that the business may well be predominantly female by the end of the century.

This turn of events, they say, could be the result of affirmative action programs. More likely it has to do with the purchasing power of today's women and their role as consumers. After all, if you're trying to project a sound corporate image to the public, you're going to have to impress the female half of the country. Perhaps that's the real reason that more than 25 percent of the members of the Public Relations Society are women.

Despite the strides women have made in this field in recent years, they still do not really do as well financially as men. Women in public relations — with the same experience and doing the same kinds of jobs as men — are not equally rewarded, according to a survey of the International Association of Business Communicators. The survey cited this example:

If you're a man editing an in-house company magazine or newspaper and have a bachelor's degree, some newspaper experience and two years in your new PR job, you'll probably make a little over $18,084. If you're a woman with exactly the same credentials, you'll only make about $14,300, according to the survey.

Want another example? Consider this: Women in the business average $18,733 a year. Men average $26,803. That's bad enough, but, according to the IABC survey, the gap appears to be growing: Men have increased their PR salaries by about 5 percent more than women in the past five years.

Nonetheless, some women *do* strike it rich in public relations. Many of them have made it to the lofty $100,000 plateau, a figure that usually includes incentive bonuses, profit sharing and pension plans.

As acceptance of the idea that women deserve equal pay for equal work grows and the number of women entering the public relations business grows, women should continue to do better and better in the business.

So will men, for that matter. This is a rapidly growing field and anyone entering it will find that out soon enough. The only direction in which to go is up.

7

Tips on Applying for Your First Job

Knowing how to handle yourself during a job interview is crucial in the public relations business. If you can't relate, you won't get the job. It's that simple.

You have to be ready to field any questions that are tossed at you. You have to anticipate.

Imagine showing up at the appointed hour to apply for a starting job as a public relations trainee at our fictitious International Widget Company.

You look terrific, you feel confident and you've made up your mind that you're going to turn in a stunning performance. Always remember, however, that confidence and neatness alone are not going to get you that job.

Maybe what you failed to do was enough research about International Widget and the job you were trying to get there. Maybe, just maybe, you don't even know what a widget is, much less what the competition is like, or how, if your luck prevails, you'll fit into the company or the corporate scheme of things.

Given all that, what do you think your chances of getting a job really are? You guessed it. Slim to nonexistent.

Your good looks, brand new clothes and vibrant personality will not get you a job. It's fine to look good, but you have to interact properly and you have to know something about the company and the industry of which it is a part.

Unintentionally, thousands of job applicants report for job interviews unprepared. In a competitive marketplace where you often have hundreds of people applying for the same job, it pays to be thoroughly prepared.

Bob Forbes, who used to be with Oxford Personnel in New York, reports that a significant number of applicants lose jobs each year because they're unprepared for the job interview.

"Other than a few highly competitive fields where applicants can name their price, today the supply often far exceeds the demand," explains Forbes. "In other words, you often have 100 applicants for the same job. In a situation like this, who do you think is going to get the job? Obviously, the applicant who makes the best impression. This is usually someone who looks good and knows something about the field he or she is trying to break into.

"Often it's not the smartest person who gets the job, but the one who is best prepared."

It all amounts to a small time investment, according to Forbes. "You'd be surprised how many applicants are shortsighted when it comes to their careers," he goes on. "An applicant will go out and buy a new suit of clothes or a new dress for an interview, yet won't invest an hour or two at the library doing research on the prospective field. Those couple of hours of research are often worth their weight in gold.

"I can't tell you how many applicants have called up confused and upset after they're turned down by a company. They were convinced they had the job in their pockets after they finished their interviews. But just because an interview went well is no guarantee you got the job. What they didn't consider was the five or six people who were interviewed after them, who were far better prepared for the interview."

There's a lot of truth to what Forbes is saying. A little time devoted to researching your career is well worth the effort in the long run.

In the process of getting a PR job, try to think of yourself as a product — a walking, talking, breathing product that has to be wrapped and packaged in such a way that you can get the job you're after. Just as a manufacturer goes out of his way to shape his product to the marketplace, you, the PR job-seeker, have to package yourself so you're just what an employer is looking for.

The first thing you have to do is study the market you hope to penetrate. In other words, where exactly are the jobs in your field? It's all well and good to say you want to promote a top computer company. But where are those computer companies you'd like to work for and how do you propose to reach them?

The worst thing you can do is to go off half-cocked without a system. In the process of studying your market, create a workable system for yourself. First identify some of the major companies in the field. This can be accomplished easily by spending some time in a main branch of your public library.

Start with PR companies you're familiar with. You can find corporate addresses plus names of top officers in *Standard & Poor's Register,* which can be found in the business section of the library.

An easy way to find out what companies dominate your field is to locate the trade associations that represent that field. This information can be found in the *Encyclopedia of Associations,* which should also be in your library.

To get specialized job information on your particular industry, get a hold of a recent edition of the *Occupational Outlook Handbook,* which is published yearly by the U.S. Department of Labor. It has fairly up-to-date information on most careers and where to get information.

Let's say you've identified the top 15 companies you might like to work for. At the end of the section on Public Relations, the *Occupational Outlook Handbook* lists some important associations that service the field and could provide you with a wealth of valuable information.

A savvy job applicant, whether he's applying for a PR job or something else, makes it a point to know as much as he or she can about the company or business before showing up for an interview. But with PR, you'd best arm yourself with information.

If you're applying by mail, write a well-thought-out letter, state your interests, tell something of your past experience, perhaps stressing a high school yearbook and/or a college newspaper . . . anything that demonstrates a writing proficiency.

But keep the letter short and to the point. No prospective employer wants to sift through a lengthy application. So, say what you have to say, and close.

Don't expect an answer by return mail. You won't get one. You're going to have to wait perhaps two weeks. If you don't receive a reply by then, you might make a polite phone call to inquire about your letter. PR firms are like any other business. Things get lost or overlooked or misplaced.

Don't be easily discouraged. If you don't get the job you've researched, don't think you've wasted your time. You've learned how to gather information and how to prepare for an interview. Chances are you'll get what you want the next time around.

What They Look For

The ideal PR person is a unique combination of both conventional and unconventional traits. Want a few of the personal characteristics that many companies look for? Here are some:

1. Outgoing nature
2. Enjoys working with people
3. Good conversationalist
4. Willingness to work hard . . . and long
5. Neat, conservative appearance
6. Assertiveness
7. Ambition
8. Success-orientation

The competition for jobs is fierce in public relations, and the sooner you realize that, the better off you'll be. Back in the 1960's, legend has it, long hair, herb tea and homegrown vegetables were the order of the day and many young people were not exactly chomping at the bit to get of out of school, go to work and buy the proverbial country house and its white picket fence.

They were quite content, 20 years ago, to see the country or travel around here and abroad, to "discover themselves." No more. The idea of life in a three-piece suit is no longer all that abhorrent.

OK, you've done your homework, you've done your research, you've got your education and you know that you really want a job in public relations. You think that you've got all the attributes that it takes to be a good PR person. So what could possibly go wrong after a little newspaper experience and the acquisition of a little expertise?

The job interview. That's what! There's an art to surviving a job interview. On one hand, the interview can land you one tremendous job. On the other, it can be a terrifying experience. If you happen to be applying for a job in public relations, you have to do a much better job of promoting yourself than if you were applying for a job, as, let's say, a bank trainee. A bank trainee doesn't really have to communicate with the public the way a public relations beginner has to. When someone goes for an interview for a job at a bank, he or she doesn't have to display the verbal skills that are expected of someone who is after a public relations job.

But a job interview is a job interview. There are all kinds of ways to make a fool of yourself. Here are a few; and though they may strike you as a trifle simplistic, they really happen:

1. Sam the Sport is really very smart. He's done well in school. He has majored in communications and he wants to go into PR. He's got all the right qualifications but he shows up in jeans and sneakers and a loud sports shirt. His interview is a disaster and he doesn't get hired, not because he isn't qualified, but because he's managed to alienate the interviewer.

2. Then there's Tom the Talker. He's bright. He has all the answers and he can talk about anything in the world. That's the problem. He talks. And talks. And talks. No one, especially in

public relations, wants just a talker, because the people who do the hiring know that being too full of words can be dangerous. In public relations, noise is not the answer. Confidence is.

Three other sins to be avoided in an interview session are arriving late for your appointment, mumbling your way through the interview and being so shy as to appear almost comatose. Again, the name of this game is communication. Tardiness, mumbling or shyness just aren't going to help you land a job . . . not in PR.

What you're actually doing in a job interview is selling yourself. It isn't all that easy to talk about your strengths without sounding like a bit of a braggart. It also isn't easy to talk about your weaknesses.

Some job experts feel a weakness can be presented so that it seems to be a strength. But don't overdo it. You can say, "My weakness is that I tend to drive myself too hard." But that way of handling the question of weaknesses can annoy an interviewer. It might be better to be honest and simply admit that sometimes you try to do too much. After all, nobody's perfect.

Almost routinely, you'll be asked what you want to be doing ten years in the future. The standard, almost cliched answer is, "I want to have your job." Don't try that on a PR person. It's far too flip and you'd be better off saying something like, "I'd like to be handling some big accounts in a field that really interests me."

Another standard question is, "Why do you want to work for our company?" You'd better have a good answer for this one, too. A really good one, if you really want the job, is: "Because of your reputation. You're one of the best PR firms in the business today."

Preparing Your Resume

There are, according to most experts, at least three different types of resumes — the chronological, the functional and the combination.

Probably the most widely accepted of these three is the chronological, mostly because interviewers are most familiar with this style. Not only that, there are a lot of advantages to presenting yourself this way and such a resume is quite easy to put together.

You simply start out by writing down your name, address and telephone number. Then you work from the present time backwards. Thus your chronological resume might look something like this:

Charles J. Jones
280 Bronxville Road
Bronxville, N.Y. 10708

Tel.: (914) 123-1234

Work Experience: Editorial assistant, monthly house organ for the XYZ Corp., New York City. Write several stories a month; handle all photo research; heavy editing on VDT screens. 1978 to present.

General assignment reporter, the *Midville Times,* Midville, N.Y., features and hard news on deadline. 1974-1978.

Education: Bronxville University, Bronxville, N.Y., B.A. in communications, 1973. Editor of college newspaper; honors graduate.

Age: 30.

References: On request.

A functional resume for the same fictional Mr. Jones might look something like the one on the following page.

Charles J. Jones
280 Bronxville Road
Bronxville, N.Y. 10708

Tel.: (914) 123-1234

Work Experience: For four years I handled all manner of
general assignment jobs for the *Midville*
(N.Y.) *Times,* many of them dealing with
corporations and their problems in the
Midville area. During that time I developed
an expertise in corporate relations and won
several awards in the business reporting field.
1974-1978.

Editorial assistant and subsequently assistant
editor of *Career Times,* a publication geared
to high school and junior college students
interested in career information. Write several
articles a month for the publication, which
has doubled its circulation since I began to
work with it. Current sales are in excess of
$100,000.
Additional duties: Photo research. Heavy
VDT machine editing. Some sales promotion.
Some personnel work. 1978 to present.

Education: Bronxville University, Bronxville, N.Y. B.A.
in communications, 1973. Editor of college
newspaper; honors graduate.

Age: 30

References: On request.

Tips on Applying for Your First Job

The functional resume, as in the preceding example, should stress specific skill areas as well as specific abilities directed toward public relations. It's a good technique to use if you happen to have a rather spotty employment record because you can camouflage a few missing dates. In the example we cited, of course, that wasn't necessary, but it's still a good technique to keep in mind.

Still using the same nonexistent Charles J. Jones of Bronxville, N.Y., here is the combination format-type resume. It's called a combination resume because it is a sort of blending of the chronological and functional resume. Generally, it highlights significant achievements and ignores earlier training, unless, of course, that's also significant.

It will look something like this:

Charles J. Jones
280 Bronxville Road
Bronxville, N.Y. 10708

Tel.: (914) 123-1234

Work experience 1978 to present:	Responsible for much of the assigning and editing of articles for a publication aimed at both high school and college students interested in obtaining career information. Involved to a large degree with market planning, merchandising and some training of sales personnel for a publication that has doubled its circulation in the four years I have been associated with it.

In addition, for this type of resume you might want to include the standard items we mentioned before: your age, education, references, etc. The loose style of the combination resume lends itself to a description of a multitude of skills.

It will work for almost any kind of job you apply for, but if it's public relations you're after, stress any kind of writing experience you can legitimately claim, even if it's only a high school newspaper or a college yearbook.

Sometimes clippings from such publications will help, although there is the story of the man who went to a PR agency with a fistful of newspaper clippings, only to be summarily asked: "How do I know you wrote all this stuff? The world is full of working editors that are paid to make you look good."

Regardless, it helps to try to build up a portfolio. If you start out in newspapers, and many public relations people seem to do that even if they do hold degrees in such things as communications or PR, save your clippings. You may run into a hardened cynic every now and then. On the other hand, you might run into someone who will be impressed with your work.

If you have some skill with a camera as well as with a typewriter, save your work, too. The more skills you can demonstrate, the better prepared you are to communicate, the more likely you are to land a decent job in this business.

8

Working Your Way Up The Corporate Ladder

Don't expect to be the head of a PR agency or top person in a corporate PR department within a couple of years. No matter how talented you are, that's an impractical goal. After coming this far, you know that there is no fast and easy road to the top.

The broad-based field of public relations is complex and multi-dimensional. There are many facets to it and it's safe to say it takes years to hone your PR skills.

There are many rungs to the PR career ladder and it's almost impossible to estimate how long it will take you to rise from one rung to the next. It depends upon individual initiative, motivation, talent, intelligence, and last but not least, good old hard work.

The big question is, "Can one start at the bottom and work his or her way to the top of the career heap?" The answer is yes. It has been done in the past and it's still being done today. New PR agencies are forming every day, small PR firms are getting bigger, and large, established ones are opening offices all over the country. And on the flip side, many well-intentioned individuals are investing large sums in new agencies and are closing their doors only months after they opened. What distinguishes the successes from the failures? No clear answer exists for this question. Suffice it to say that the successful in the field were clever enough to proceed cautiously, moving up the ladder step by step. They weighed each move carefully and they proceeded when they were sure of what was ahead. In short, there were no surprises for them. They never doubted they would accomplish their goals.

"There are no shortcuts to learning the business," said the owner of a small, established Chicago PR firm. "I got my first PR job when I was 23, and I didn't open up my own firm until I was 40. I know a lot of people who started their own agencies when they were in their late 20s and 30s. However, many of those firms failed because the owners weren't ready to head their own operations. Looking back, I could have started a small firm much earlier in my career. But it would have been a risky venture. I don't know whether I would have made it or not. The key word here is *experience*. I had the contacts, know-how and talent behind me. When I did make my move, I never doubted that I would succeed. I was ready."

Experience Counts

Just like any other field, experience in PR is a crucial ingredient to landing a high-paying job with potential. Look at the employment ads for public relations jobs in your daily newspaper. The higher the salary, the more experience they're looking for.

The important question is how one gets experience and what kind of job experience will be most valuable. That's another difficult question with no simple answer. The best way to answer it is to ease into it. Typically, there are two paths into public relations, the *direct path* and the *indirect path*. The direct path is the logical career path from college right into a public relations firm. Those taking the direct path are in touch with their career objectives early in their careers. They've majored in public relations or a related field like communications in college and, after graduating, they step right into an apprentice position in a general PR agency or possibly a large corporate PR department.

The indirect path, as you've probably guessed, is the unconventional route. It is, in fact, the route taken by the majority of people interviewed earlier in the book. Here backgrounds vary and the circumstances leading into the field are different.

An experienced journalist with 20 years on a large metropolitan daily joins a PR firm as a highly paid writer, or a chemist with impressive educational credentials who worked for a major chemical company for a number of years joins a PR firm specializing in chemical accounts as an account executive.

Or a writer who spent a number of years working on a monthly trade magazine for the cosmetics industry joins the PR department of a cosmetics firm as a coordinating editor of a house organ. There are many more examples that could be cited. The essential difference between the two routes is that in the indirect route your prior work and educational background are the important criteria guiding you into public relations work. After working in a closely related field you decide that public relations work, which adapts the skills and techniques you've learned working in another business sphere, would be more to your liking. So for those who wander into PR jobs via the indirect route, their career paths are pretty clear to them. They know where they are going and how to best put their talent to work.

However, the path isn't so clear for those starting off with very little or no experience in the field. Trying to pick the right type of organization to work for is a crucial career decision. To illustrate this point, picture this situation: You're about to graduate from a PR degree program in a couple of months and you're already considering a number of interesting job opportunities in the following areas: government, small PR firm, large tire company, labor union or PR department of a conglomerate.

Imagine the frustration of not knowing which job to take. Each job seems attractive to you, yet you're hard-pressed to find an easy way out of the dilemma. You have no experience in the field and no particular career goals. Which job should our imaginary trainee take? If you were in the same position, what would you do?

If you picked the conglomerate, you made a sound choice. Since you have no strong feelings as to which PR field you'd eventually like to be working in a decade from now, your best bet is a job offering a smattering of different public relations fields and skills — a position where you're not dealing with one particular product or service, but many.

Working for the conglomerate would offer you just such an opportunity. The conglomerate in question is a large corporate empire with offices all over the world. It's involved not in 1 business but in 12 major business sectors, each of which is a separate entity unto itself. It employs a PR staff that could be compared to that of a sizable public relations firm. The position is public relations trainee.

As a trainee you'll be spending a number of months in every major PR department. At the end of a 12-month training period you'll be placed in a department which will best utilize your skills and career inclinations. And beyond that, there are many career options open for you. A year or two later you might find that a transfer to a new department is a compatible career move.

No matter how you look at it, you've made the right choice. But if you had taken a job with the tire company, small PR firm or labor union, your career options would have been restricted. Government and labor union public relations, as we said earlier, are highly specialized fields with unique problems and goals. Working for a tire company limits you to one business area, and working for a small PR firm again restricts you to a firm that services only a handful of accounts. So you see, each of these job experiences is limiting in its own way.

Which Path Shall I Take?

You should know the answer to that one now. Initially, the best career path is one offering a variety of choices. In the example above, we cited the conglomerate as a good example of a company offering a broad-based experience of what public relations work is all about. In other words, a general background in many public relations areas is the ideal foundation for building a career that can ultimately take off in many different directions.

Many college graduates try to secure jobs with one of the many large public relations firms where the opportunities for advancement are virtually unlimited. Not everyone knows what skill-area they'd like to pursue. You might be interested in two areas — writing and working as an account executive. If you're working for a large agency, you stand a good chance of doing both.

Keep in mind that there are also advantages to working for a small firm. In a ten-person firm, for example, you'll get the opportunity to do a little bit of everything. When you're not preparing press releases and media kits, for example, you'll be working directly with clients and planning promotional campaigns. In a small firm you have little choice but to wear many hats.

Ultimately, however, your long-range advancement potential is limited. Or, technically speaking, your vertical mobility is restricted by the size of the company. If you're a junior PR worker involved with our fictitious ten-person staff, it's going to take a lot longer for you to move up the career ladder.

Since there are other junior PR writers and account executives who have seniority over you, you'll have to wait your turn before advancing to the next career notch. Not so with a large public relations agency. In a PR firm employing hundreds of workers, the path to the top is wide-open and clear.

Companies like that are constantly taking on new accounts, and there is a perpetual flow of new workers coming and going within any given year. If you're unsure of what area you'd like to concentrate on, you can get your feet wet by sampling different departments. There is no better way to understand how a PR agency works than by working for a number of major departments.

Many junior PR workers start off in the research department and then eventually move into the editorial and publicity departments. And others wander through several departments before settling into the account executive or administrative end of the business.

Research is part of moving up the corporate ladder. (Photo courtesy of Vista)

Generalist Versus Specialist

After getting an all-purpose background in public relations work, several years down the road, you'll be equipped to decide whether you want to be a generalist or a specialist.

Many PR workers, for example, prefer to work on a variety of accounts. They enjoy working with a clothing manufacturer part of the time and dividing their attention among paper products, food and toy companies the rest of the time. They enjoy the challenge of working with companies in different industries, while others would rather concentrate their energy on one particular area.

In the technical sector, you might want to spend the majority of your time working exclusively with engineering companies. Here you're limiting yourself to a specialized area, yet your chances for advancement are excellent as long as you confine yourself to this field. Specialists in any field are usually well paid.

Formulating Sensible Career Goals

Only when you've gotten a taste of public relations work can you formulate realistic career goals. Some people know exactly what they want after working for a company for a couple of years, while others need at least four to five years before they can formulate realistic career goals. There is no time limit for setting these goals.

It depends upon you. The idea is to create goals that are compatible with your personality, motivations and emotional constitution. Not all of us are going to own PR agencies and not everyone is going to earn $100,000 a year either. Goals are relative and personal and it's important to be aware of that from the start.

It takes a special blend of talent and drive to own your own agency. Aside from having a solid understanding of how a public relations firm functions, you also have to be ready to make the time investment. As we said in prior chapters, PR workers rarely work conventional hours. But as owner of your own agency, you can realistically expect to be working around the clock until your company is launched and functioning on its own.

Your goal should be to find that special niche within public relations that allows you to work to your full potential. Most established PR writers, for instance, couldn't imagine doing anything but concentrating on honing their writing skills. And, as you already know, the writing spectrum within the PR field is quite broad. Take PR writers specializing in annual report or speech writing. Both of these areas are highly specialized and require skilled practitioners. Annual report writing, for one, requires a deft writing style, a good financial background and an understanding of editorial production. And speech writing is a skill all by itself. Corporate and political speech writers can name their price. It's not uncommon for a speech writer to earn $50,000 a year, and sometimes more. They perform an essential skill and it's common practice for one company to bid for a favored speech writer in order to lure him or her from one corporate camp to another. Corporate speech writers enjoy the unique position of being able to leave one job and walk right into another.

Most speech writers, along with most highly prized PR practitioners, are content to remain where they are and perfect their talents and skills to the best of their abilities.

It's important not to set unrealistic goals for yourself. Keep in mind that everyone moves at his or her own pace. Just as we all walk at different speeds, we all move up the career ladder at a pace that is comfortable and compatible with our own natures. It might take your best friend two years to move from the position of junior writer to that of senior writer, while it might take you twice as long.

Time is not the crucial factor here. What is important is moving ahead at the right time, and only when you've mastered a particular skill. Your long-range goal should be to be totally proficient within your career area. If you accomplish that, you are realizing your career objective.

A workable suggestion is to set approximate goals for yourself. This way you can tailor your goals to your job situation. Once you've gotten a feeling of what PR work is all about, set up a goal chart for yourself. Two possibilities are the vertical and horizontal charts.

First the vertical chart. If you're working towards being the editorial coordinator or editor in chief of your company's editorial department, for instance, list all the job rungs you have to climb to reach that goal. If you're an editorial researcher, which puts you pretty close to the bottcm of the career ladder, you might have to move ten job slots to reach your goal. Your chart might look something like this:

Goal Chart

10	Long-Term Goal	Editor in chief (8 to 10 years)
9		
8		
7		
6		
5	Intermediate-Term Goal	Senior Writer (3 to 5 years)
4		
3		
2		Junior Writer
1		

It's best to be as explicit as possible. Clearly outline the path ahead of you, and then list each job slot. This way you know what's ahead of you and what has to be done to achieve your goal. It leaves nothing to chance. Also estimate how long you think it will take to reach each goal step. Again, it is only an approximation and a gauge. Since each goal step is numbered, each time you achieve a goal, cross it off your list. Every six months to a year, take a look at your goal chart and revise it accordingly.

An even simpler goal chart is the horizontal chart which is merely a variation on the vertical chart. A horizontal chart looks something like this:

Goal Path

Junior Writer	Goal	(Editor in chief)
~~1~~ ~~2~~ ~~3~~ ~~4~~ 5 6 7 8 9	10	

Each time a goal step is reached, cross it off by putting a line through it as shown in the illustration. With the horizontal goal chart, you're not restricting yourself to a set time period. When your goal destination is reached, create another chart for yourself with a new set of goals.

Goals are important in any field, but they're especially important in an enormous profession like public relations, where there are so many career paths at your disposal. Remember, having a goal orientation is important. It roots you to a time and place and structures your career path. It also permits you to analyze your progress and achieve a better understanding of the field you're trying to conquer. By monitoring your goal path, for example, you might discover that there is a more direct path to your goal, or possibly that you've taken the wrong path unknowingly. With a little thought and reflection, you can reorient yourself and proceed along a new career path.

Evaluating Yourself and Moving Up the Ladder

A common question often asked by junior PR workers is "When is the opportune time to make a career move?" This could mean changing jobs within your own firm or moving to a new firm at a higher salary.

Unfortunately, there is no all-purpose answer to this question either. Suffice it to say that it depends solely on you and your career potential within your company. If you're working for a large public relations firm, it makes little sense to move to another firm when you think you're ready to take on more responsibility. If you're content with your company and there is room for growth, stay where you are and make the most out of an opportune situation. As far as when to take the career initiative: personal initiative is important and respected, especially in a field like public relations that rewards "take charge," highly motivated workers.

If your supervisor fails to recognize your talents and doesn't recommend you for a promotion, make your thoughts known. Speak to your supervisor or the assistant vice-president and tell him how you feel. See what they have to say. If they agree with you, you will have succeeded in pulling yourself up by your own bootstraps, so to speak. If the powers that be don't feel you're ready to take on more responsibility, you're faced with an important decision: Either wait until you're promoted to a new job, or look elsewhere for a new job. Decisions like this will have to be made throughout your career. This involves some serious thought, considering the pros and cons of either leaving or staying, and the possible advantages of obtaining a better job with another firm.

Like advertising, public relations workers tend to change jobs several times throughout their careers. Very often, PR workers are excessed (that's the polite way of saying they've been fired) through no fault of their own. An all-too-common occurrence is when the PR firm you're working for loses the account which you happen to be working on. All of a sudden, you serve no purpose, and the company politely terminates your employment. Or, you might be the victim of a reorganization. This means your department was restructured to cut costs and increase efficiency, and in the process, they found you expendable. Again, because of situations beyond your control, you're forced to find a new place to ply your trade.

However, it makes little sense to change jobs for no reason. Keep in mind that the average American changes jobs about six or more times throughout a career. For PR workers it's a lot higher. Before moving to a new position, weigh the advantages and disadvantages carefully. Ask yourself these questions:

1. What do I stand to benefit from changing jobs?
2. What are my growth prospects if I remain at my present job?
3. Will my long-term objectives be met by changing jobs?

If you can find clear-cut answers to the above questions, you'll know exactly what career move to make.

As one placement manager with a New York-based employment agency said: "You can't be shortsighted when it comes to changing jobs. I've seen too many people change jobs for a salary increase alone. Not that money isn't important. It certainly is. But you have to take the long-term view and ask yourself where your greatest growth prospects are.

"I've seen many situations where it pays to take a slight salary cut, in order to reap substantial rewards down the road. It's not easy, but you have to be very objective when it comes to changing jobs. Money should never be the sole reason for changing positions. Ideally, there should be a combination of factors which makes a career move necessary."

As a rough guide, it pays to remain at your first job at least one year before considering changing jobs. And after that, it pays to be safe and weigh the situation carefully before making a move.

Analyzing the Market

Even though you're safe and secure in an established firm, and your growth prospects are assured, don't lose touch with the marketplace. You don't have to be actively looking for another position in your free time, but it's to your advantage to keep an eye on the public relations market. This is important for estimating your own worth. Your value is gauged by the law of supply and demand. And salaries are set by this irrefutable economic law. If your talent is in short supply, you can command a higher price in the marketplace. On the other hand, if you're one of millions, your bargaining potential is limited.

One agency head referred to the competitive public relations job market as a giant chessboard. "The smart ones learn never to take their eyes off the board. In other words, know what's out there, who's paying what and where the good jobs are."

In terms of judging your own worth and marketability, make it a point to keep a watchful eye on your field. Who knows, without warning you too might be excessed or become the victim of a departmental reorganization. If one of these events should happen, you'll be able to cope with the news and act accordingly. Having monitored the job market all along, you'll be equipped and ready to move on to an equally lucrative, if not better, job situation.

9

The Future of Public Relations

The future of public relations, the fine art of persuasive communication, is virtually unlimited. Considering the fact that 50 years ago this was an art of which no one had heard, the field has come a long way.

The nature and purpose of public relations may still be a bit misunderstood, but most well-informed people anywhere are surely aware of the profession's existence. Rest assured, PR is here to stay.

It's one of the fastest growing fields in the world. Virtually no one is untouched by the art of the PR professional — from businessperson to corporate executive to politician.

Over and over again we have used the word communication. As man's ability to communicate via the written word, satellite or television expands, more and more we are going to be bombarded with corporate messages designed to heighten our perceptions of a particular company, policy or country.

Therefore, more and more people are going to be hired to work in this field. It's glamorous. It's exciting. It pays well. It is plainly going to attract a lot of people with a lot of talent. What's also plain is that the competition for such jobs is going to get tougher and tougher.

That's because the entire art of communication demands highly skilled people, no matter how they start out.

You may never wind up owning your own public relations firm. That's not a very realistic goal although it has been reached by many people. But you can make a far better than average living in this field.

One of the things to keep in mind is the reality of this business. Yes, you have to be smart. Yes, you have to be able to communicate on many different levels. Yes, you have to be something of a salesperson, something of an orator.

It's a field that demands specific communication skills. It doesn't really matter how you acquire them — at a college or on a newspaper — but acquire them you must.

No one who's worked for any length of time in this business would quarrel with the notion that there's still a lot of room for improvement, a lot of areas in which the pros who practice this art — and it is an art — could do better. Here are a few examples:

1. Getting employers to understand. Everyone in business, as well as in many other areas, has begun to realize in recent years the importance of employing skilled communicators. But there are limitations to what PR can accomplish.

Getting your message across properly can take time. You can't leave such a program for the last minute. Sometimes you'll use the written word. Other times you'll use everything from film strips to public lectures or TV appearances. Convincing corporations of the complexities of mass communications, the need for mass communications and the limitations of mass communications constitutes a PR job in itself.

2. Improved understanding of the world around us. Public relations people must develop a better understanding of why people think the way they do. If they don't, they're going to have major problems in getting their messages across.

3. Education. There is still a great deal of disagreement about the value of a public relations curriculum in college. Hundreds of schools teach courses in what they are fond of calling "communications." Sometimes they use the more straightforward words, "public relations." But what, ask the doubters, are they really teaching? Of what, if any, value is it?

Perhaps the quality of the PR education could use some examination and some improvement. Slowly but surely, that's what is happening.

4. Global contacts. This is an international business, which comprises travel and relationships with people in other countries. It no longer is a uniquely American endeavor.

Ours is a world of almost instant communications and multinational corporations that buy and sell their goods in dozens of different nations. This is something that the public relations person of the future is going to have to learn to adjust to.

5. Ethics. It's odd that a profession devoted to creating an image for a person, place, thing, company or country should have an image problem itself. If you say PR to a lot of people, they'll smile at you in a rather deprecating manner. They'll put it down.

That is going to have to change if this industry is to continue to grow. Those who practice it in the future are going to have to develop a greater sense of conscience. If they don't, the public will not accept the messages PR workers are paid to put across.

In essence, the public relations industry is really going to have to sell itself. It is going to have to use PR to sell PR to the American public.

6. PR and government. In this area the responsibility is almost staggering. Public relations in government, be it local, statewide, federal or international, is potentially an instrument of vast power. That power is going to increase. It cannot be disguised, nor can its abuse be excused.

Information is one thing. Distortion is another. Therefore the question of ethics is going to arise again and again. Here, perhaps, is a role especially suited to colleges and universities — pioneering the exploration of ethical issues.

Go back and reread Chapter One of this book. In it, we discussed the tremendous growth of big business and the vast changes in the communications process over the last two or three decades alone.

That's going to affect anyone contemplating a career in public relations. You communicate a lot differently today than you did 30 years ago. Your methods of communication are different. So are your abilities to communicate.

But the principles aren't going to change. You are always going to have to attract people's attention and hold it. To do that, you're going to have to use different methods. Radio and newspapers may help you achieve that. But they won't be enough.

You're going to have to master the electronic media, because that's going to be the quickest and most efficient way to get your message across. Perhaps communications wouldn't be a bad major in college, after all.

One other thing that maybe you should keep in mind: Salaries are bound to go up. People who are paid $20,000, $30,000 and $40,000 nowadays will be paid twice as much in the future.

They'd better have twice the skills, because they'll need them. They'll need them whether they're communicating internally or externally.

While public relations is still a very young field, relatively speaking, the operative words, the key words, remain the same.

They are: influence, persuasion, convince, and attention. We're not saying that if they are all paid attention to that success will automatically follow.

But it sure can't hurt!

Index